The Garland Library of War and Peace

The Garland Library of War and Peace

The New Cineas

by

Eméric Crucé

(Eméric La Croix)

translated, with an introduction
for the Garland Edition by

C. Frederick Farrell, Jr.
and
Edith R. Farrell

Garland Publishing, Inc., New York & London
1972

Library of Congress Cataloging in Publication Data

Crucé, Émeric, 1590-1648.
The new Cineas.

(The Garland library of war and peace)
Translation of Le nouveau Cynée.
Bibliography: p.
1. Economics. 2. Arbitration, International.
3. Free trade and protection--Free trade. 4. Peace.
I. Title. II. Series.
HB153.C7813 1972 330 75-147415
ISBN 0-8240-0213-X

Printed in the United States of America

Introduction

Eméric Crucé tells us little about his life, and history has been able to add only a few details. In The New Cineas *Crucé declares himself to be French and Catholic; the title page bears the signature* Em. Cr. Par., *making it clear that the author considers himself a Parisian. This is all he reveals directly.*

Other information has been gathered from fragments: anagrams and insults written during a literary quarrel with Gronovius the Elder, ink-written notations on the flyleaves of books, and conjectures for which supporting evidence was found in documents of the times.

He was born in 1590, perhaps near Blois. He was a monk, probably a Célestin, who lived in Paris where he taught in a collège. *From his writings we know him to be a man of learning. In 1648 he died of a liver ailment and was buried, according to his wishes, in the cemetery near "Cardinalitios" on December 6. The epitaph he chose affirms his faith in God and also in his name on which his detractors had cast reflections. It reads:*

> *Spes christiana quae dedit nomen mihi,*
> *Det nunc salutem: vota jam testor mea;*
> *Junge his, viator, si vacat, preces tuas:*

INTRODUCTION

Sic sospitet te, vota fortunans tua,
*Spes christiana quae dedit nomen mihi.**

Even his name has posed a problem. In Latin works, including bibliographies, there are different spellings of Emericus Cruceus. The difficulty was compounded when these versions were retranslated into French. In all, there exist at least six variants of his first name; eight of his last.[1] *It was not until 1890 that Ernest Nys established Eméric Crucé as his true name.*[2]

These meager indications we owe to the patient scholarship, not only of Ernest Nys, but also of Milan R. Vesnitch and Pierre Louis-Lucas.[3]

Crucé's writings were, for the most part, literary. He wrote three eulogies to the kings in whose reigns he lived: Adonia seu Mnomosynon Henrici Magni *(1613),* Soteria Casalea, sive expeditio Italica Ludovici Justi *(1620), and* Justa Ludovici Justi, Franciae et Navarrae regis christianissimi *(1642). He also produced two commentaries on the works of Statius:* Publii Papinii Statii opera *(1618) and* Notae in Statii Thebaïdos *(1620).*

The works of literary criticism were not well received either by his contemporaries or by later

**O hope of Christians which gave my name to me,*
Now grant salvation: I here set forth my wishes;
Join to my prayers your own, passer-by, if there be time:
Thus may you be sustained and all your prayers be granted, through
That hope of Christians which gave my name to me.

scholars.[4] *They are important to us only in that they precipitated a violent literary quarrel with Gronovius the Elder, who wrote two attacks on Crucé, thereby bringing the latter to public notice. Crucé responded to each attack with his* P. Papinii Statii silvarum frondatio sive antidiatribe *(1639) and* Emerici Crucei ad P. Papinii Statii silvas muscarium sive Helelenchus *(1640) respectively.*

None of these biographical or bibliographical data prepare us for the appearance in 1623 of a work of the scope and vision of The New Cineas. *Here is the work not of an obscure monk or schoolmaster with a limited outlook on the world, nor of a literary critic whose tastes are aesthetic and whose preoccupations are far from the realm of practical realities. Here, on the contrary, we find the work of a man who addresses himself to most of the major political, social, economic, and religious issues of his day and of the centuries to come. Issues, moreover, whose proposed resolutions form an integral plan for the amelioration of the condition of man and are based on a philosophy that has become more and more widely accepted as the world has moved toward the concept of oneness that Crucé envisioned.*

The New Cineas *was received enthusiastically at the time, witness a second edition within a year. Today only a few copies remain. Yet despite the fact that the book became rare and that the author was virtually unknown until recently, Crucé's wish that his work would "find a place in the libraries of great men"*[5] *seems to have been realized.*

What are the major virtues that have caused The New Cineas *to be rescued time after time from threatened oblivion?*

Certainly the central issue, the one around which all the rest revolves, is Crucé's plan for a world-wide peace organization. Although the idea of international arbitration was not new, Crucé's plan was different from any other put forth. His great originality lies, first of all, in the fact that every independent government in the world, without exception, is urged to join. Secondly, his proposed organization is a permanent body of ambassadors able to give immediate attention to any disagreements that might arise. A third crucial point is his advocacy of sanctions. Although he hopes that all nations will learn to think as one, Crucé is realistic enough to provide for other contingencies. He stresses diplomacy through the agreement among nations to establish diplomatic and economic sanctions and finally to use armed intervention, should all else fail.

Once this system becomes operative, Crucé believes, there will be universal peace; and each individual state will be better able, not only to function effectively, but to work actively for the betterment of its own people and of all mankind.

On the level of domestic affairs, Crucé touches only upon those policies that he deems essential for good government. Specifically, he discusses the need for "moderate government, the punishment of wickedness, reward for good, provision for the poor, the regulation of trials, public provision of grain, lawful recreation and the power of censure. A state," he says, "is healthy when all of these conditions are met" (p. 86). Many of the ideas found in this section of the Cineas *had already been stated by Jean Bodin.*[6] *Crucé's merit lay chiefly in recognizing their value and in refusing to follow blindly even an authority of Bodin's stature. When Crucé disagrees with him, he rarely indulges in polemics, but never hesitates to put forth an opposing view.*[7]

In keeping with his avowed aim of establishing and maintaining peace, both at home and abroad, Crucé propounds a doctrine of religious tolerance far in advance of his times. He sees religious differences as having served only as a pretext for war and internal factions. He believes that basically "they [religions] all strive for the same end, namely the recognition and adoration of a divinity" (p. 50). While maintaining that there is one true religion, Crucé considers that knowledge of it is dependent solely on God's grace and that men should neither scorn nor use force on non-believers, unless they constitute a threat to the state.

Economics, too, plays a vital role in Crucé's plan for universal peace. He is aware that poverty and despair lead men to crimes within the state and wars among nations. His doctrine of free-trade, liberal even by twentieth-century standards, is remarkable for his time. He favors the abolition of duties on imported goods, except for a moderate tax, imposed equally on natives and foreigners, for the maintenance of the treasury. He sees clearly that such a policy would be beneficial to everyone. The merchants would increase in number when they could trade freely and without fear; every state would have a sufficient supply of all commodities and a stable revenue; and the people could buy goods at a lower price.

It is important to note, however, that, while these ideas may seem idle dreams or impossibilities given conditions in 1623, Crucé does not consider them as such. "Nothing is impossible, he declares, if men are willing to work at it" (p. 39). Knowing that some "who lack sufficient insight" (p. VIII) would compare his work to Plato's Republic *or other plans that work only on paper, Crucé is careful, both by the examples he cites and by the practical details he provides, to show how universal peace* can *be realized.*

Crucé's conviction that universal peace can be attained and perpetuated is based, at least in part, on his belief in men's common humanity. "There is a kind of friendship and kinship among men that springs from the basic similarity in their nature and physical appearance" (p. 5). Inhumanity is the worst and most basic vice. If it can be destroyed, universal peace will result. In Crucé's opinion the majority of men will support the side of good, are by nature social and hospitable, and want peace. While he decries the many backslidings of particular men or groups of men, still their basic goodness will triumph, if only the suitable first steps can be taken.

The word "harmony" is fundamental to Crucé, and it is an important one to bear in mind while reading The New Cineas. *This harmony is shown in the complete interdependence of the component parts of his plan. It reflects the state that he hopes the world will achieve, i.e., universal peace and understanding. It underlies the spirit of moderation that is everywhere to be seen in both the theories and practices that he recommends. The basic value of harmony so permeates his thought that it influences him even in such relatively minor subjects as suitable forms of recreation. He chooses music as the most valid, feeling that men will be drawn naturally to its harmony and profit from contact with it.*

What of the influences that may have lead Crucé to these conclusions? This is a complex and uncertain subject, on which there is disagreement among scholars.

Much of the difficulty stems from the number of subjects discussed in this relatively small book. In addition, most of them are questions with which both ordinary men and philosophers had already struggled for centuries. To trace the development of all of them – even to give an annotated list of all the books Crucé might *have consulted, since there is no doubt that he was well-read – would be a monumental task.*

Therefore, we shall mention only two major works and, briefly, some significant events of the period in which Crucé wrote. Vesnitch considers Eméric

Crucé's work to be a clear outgrowth of that of Pierre Dubois (or Petrus de Bosco), who, in 1305, wrote De recuperatione terrae Sanctae.[8] *Vesnitch's work also provides a brief background on other writers who study government, peace, and society,*[9] *but he believes Dubois to be of primary importance. He bases his conclusion on Dubois's feeling for the concept of nationalism, his effort to unite Christian rulers, his concept of international arbitration, his desire for a lasting peace, and his idea of a council of rulers to lead the world and to form an international court of arbitration.*

Louis-Lucas disagrees with this position. He finds the resemblances between Dubois and Crucé completely artificial. He points to the differences in their motives and goals to substantiate his contentions.[10] *Dubois valued power for France, national sovereignty above international goals, and control by threat of excommunication rather than by diplomacy. His major aim was uniting the Christians* against *the Moslems to recover the Holy Land. While Louis-Lucas freely grants that Dubois was ahead of his time, he thinks that Crucé was even further ahead of his.*

Louis-Lucas believes that Crucé was influenced first by facts and events, secondly by doctrines, and thirdly by his personal convictions.[11] *He concludes that those who wrote before Crucé were merely predecessors rather than direct sources of inspiration, since* The New Cineas *is the very antithesis of an erudite compilation of historical arguments.*[12] *The exception to this statement, according to Louis-Lucas, is Jean Bodin whose work,* Les six livres de la République *(1577), was used by Crucé as a starting point for his views on domestic affairs. Bodin is the one contemporary writer named in* The New Cineas, *and Crucé's theory of "moderate government" is Bodin's concept. Many of Crucé's opinions on social institutions were likewise affirmations of Bodin's positions. Louis-Lucas hastens to point out, however, that Crucé never adopts anything merely on authority. First, it has to be analyzed and approved by his own critical faculties. He disagrees with Bodin, for example, on the legitimacy of tyrannicide, on the extent to which arbitration is feasible, on whether war has any redeeming features, on the value of the theater, and on other points.*[13]

Crucé does not mention current history, preferring to find parallels in the experience of the Ancients, at whom, presumably, everyone could look more objectively, or perhaps, as Louis-Lucas suggests, because of the authority which their words and examples had long had.[14] *Still, given the nature of Crucé's preoccupations, and the events of the period during which he lived and wrote, it is impossible not to believe that he was suggesting remedies for situations that he had observed personally.*

Louis-Lucas believes that the events of his own lifetime were the strongest influence on Crucé's political and economic thought.[15] *Crucé had already seen the effects of the reign of Henry IV, the*

Regency, and the first years of Louis XIII. It was a time of wars and uprisings at home and abroad, brought about by both political and religious issues. At the time of The New Cineas, *the Thirty Years' War was expanding and threatening France.*

Henry IV had been a strong and successful king. He and his minister, Sully, were remembered for military victories, for their desire to create a balance of power in Europe by reducing the power of the Empire, for their efforts to improve industry and commerce, for the Edict of Nantes, and for their desire for a lasting peace. (Rumors of a "Grand Design" that would bring about world peace had circulated constantly since Henry's death.)

On the other hand, Crucé had seen the weak government of the Regency: the revolts led by the League in the early seventeenth century, and a decline of France's status in Europe both politically and economically. At this moment of domestic unrest, the threat of the Thirty Years' War, low morale among the people, and the clearly visible effects of war and devastation in Europe; and before the strong leadership of Richelieu could restore France's prestige, Crucé worked out his plan. It was "entirely original because it is the first really to deserve the name."[16]

While Crucé omits mention of France's own difficulties, we are not surprised to find an indictment of civil uprisings, a plea for a stable economy, guidelines for an able ruler, and, most important, a well-organized plan for perpetual peace. Although Crucé's plans needed time to be realized, and although he remained in relative obscurity for two hundred years, those who did know of The New Cineas *generally spoke favorably of it and of its author, even if they were often doubtful about the possibility of the success of such novel policies.*

In the seventeenth century, for example, Gabriel Naudé in La Bibliographie politique *(1642) mentions: "Emery de la Croix, a Parisian, [and] . . . the book* The New Cineas, *which he wrote more in the spirit of mental relaxation than in any real conviction that his opinion might prevail."* [17] *Charles Sorel, in 1664, adds: "There is a book entitled* The New Cineas *which gives advice on establishing a general peace and freedom of trade throughout the world. It seems hardly likely that it could succeed as it stands; still, the concept is both admirable and courageous."* [18]

In the eighteenth century Leibnitz wrote (1714) "When still very young, I knew of a book entitled The New Cineas *whose unknown author advised rulers to govern their states in peace and to submit their differences to an established tribunal; but I no longer know where to find this book; and I don't remember any of its details."* [19] *Leibnitz's comment may seem insignificant in itself. However, it had a far-reaching effect, since it appears to have been the starting point for Nys's work on Crucé.*[20]

In the middle of the eighteenth century Réal de Curban wrote in his Science du gouvernement

"Emeri de la Croix is the first writer who conceived a plan for perpetual peace among all the princes of the world, not a very sensible plan, if indeed it is anything but a joke." [21]

Another century elapsed before there appeared in 1839 an anonymous article in the Magasin pittoresque *entitled "Utopistes célèbres." This author said of Crucé, "of all the thinkers who occupied their leisure time in constructing a hypothetical future of peace, order, and happiness for Nations, none, perhaps, saw further or more clearly than he." Speaking of Crucé's support of the merchant, "these principles are completely new at the dawn of the seventeenth century; what follows is even more so . . . [Crucé's doctrine of free-trade]. These are the counsels of a wise economist; how many times since 1623 have they not been presented to all governments, to both monarchies and republics? And still they have yet to be followed."* [22] *This unknown author also recognized Crucé's abilities in other fields. "As a statesman, he is ahead of his contemporaries by several hundred years in revealing a future based on an order and peace that neither the Treaties of Westphalia nor the Congress of Vienna have yet accomplished."* [23]

Crucé is next mentioned in a speech by Charles Sumner before the American Peace Society in May, 1849.[24] *Then another anonymous article appeared in the* Eclectic Review *in August of the same year. Its author, who had been allowed to examine Mr. George Sumner's copy of* The New Cineas, *says of Crucé:*

"On the question of free trade and religious liberty, as well as that of peace, the author seems to have been greatly in advance of his age."[25] *Later that same month (on August 22) at the Peace Conference of Paris, presided over by Victor Hugo and Richard Cobden, a paper was read that told of Sumner's discovery of a copy of* The New Cineas.[26]

Since Mr. Nys's discovery of the authorship of The New Cineas *in 1890, more studies have been published. Many of these are listed in the Bibliographies of the present volume. These authors retain the admiration of earlier writers for Crucé but have lost much of the scepticism of previous centuries, since they have seen more and more of Crucé's ideas realized or at least widely recognized as both desirable and possible. Nys himself said of Crucé in 1890, "He has great scope of vision. He is an enemy of war, and his work is as well written as it is nobly thought out."*[27] *Thomas Balch in his introduction to* The New Cineas *in 1909 comments on some reasons for Crucé's having less influence than other writers. "Crucé's bolder and more practical plan . . . took longer to mature than the more general idea of Grotius, and it was not until two and three-quarter centuries [later] . . . that it was realized as a result of the labors of the First Hague Peace Conference."*[28] *Daniel Crick admires Crucé, finding "proof in his analysis of this question [religion] of a spirit of tolerance and a 'generosity' which, given the times in which he wrote and the author's status as a religious, are worthy of admiration."*[29] *Vesnitch summarizes him, in 1911, in these words, "Today it is definitely established that Crucé was a man of great worth, a talented writer and a thinker who was far ahead of his time."*[30] *Louis-Lucas (1919) praises him because "In small questions as in large, with regard to details as well as principles, Crucé gave evidence of broad penetrating foresight."*[31] *"He did better than inspire the generations immediately following him to adopt his tastes; he defined the aspirations of men of today, separated from him by three centuries."*[32] *Sir Geoffrey Butler (1920) pays tribute, among other things, to his vast learning. "In the original the treatment is immense, all history is ransacked for arguments, the Bible, Justinian, French provincial customs, Bodin's writings. . . ."*[33]

Mention should be made of Crucé's style. The lengthy sentences and paragraphs of the period may bother the modern reader. The criticism has also been made that he wanders. Louis-Lucas attributes this seeming fault to the very complex interrelationship of all the parts of the whole. Everything may be brought into focus, however, by considering the relationship of each part to Crucé's guiding philosophy.[34]

Crucé's style has been compared to that of Montaigne. Neither of them overstresses the moral, but it is nonetheless profound. They both use simple but striking images and make constant allusions to the Ancients. The two differ in that Montaigne wrote for himself whereas Crucé directed his efforts to the needs of others.[35]

Flashes of wit and irony enliven the reading of The New Cineas, *e.g., "Titus said that no man should leave the presence of a prince dissatisfied. Things are very different today, for there is usually sufficient reason to be unhappy before ever speaking to the prince" (p. 132).*

Crucé also has the talent for shocking even a twentieth-century reader with a remark so strikingly true that it might have been in the day's paper, e.g., ". . . you end up losing the benefits of a hard-won conquest which is ordinarily more expensive than if you had just bought the land outright" (p. 55).

Descriptive passages are one of his favorite devices for convincing his readers, e.g., his description of the horrors of war. "Let us imagine two armies ready to clash with each other, the looks of fury, the hideous faces of the soldiers, the threats, the barbarous cries coming from both sides, mingled with the thundering of the canon: then the charge, the frightful mêlée, a slaughter of men, some dismembered, others half dead and imploring their comrades to help them by finishing them off so as to cut short the torment of their miserable, ebbing lives" (p. 223).

Although those who knew the work praised it, for the most part, the question must be raised as to whether or not The New Cineas *had a direct influence on the thinking of subsequent writers. During his lifetime, it seems fairly certain that it did.*[36]

Hugo Grotius, who published his De jure belli ac

pacis *in Paris (1625, reprinted in The Garland Library of War and Peace, 1972) must certainly have known of Crucé. First, because he had come to Paris for the purpose of studying the question of relationships among governments, and Crucé's book was published during this period. Secondly, because he had a close relationship with Gronovius, he would surely have known of the literary quarrel over Statius, and therefore of Crucé. Grotius sought primarily to moderate and alleviate the suffering caused by war, which he thought was a normal phenomenon in human affairs and sometimes justified. But, here and there, pacifist ideas and the concept of arbitration (at least among Christian rulers) come out in a book whose author believes war inevitable. Louis-Lucas has discovered that there is one entire chapter where the idea, tone, and style are so radically different that it seems to be Crucé and not Grotius who is speaking.* [37]

Sully, whose memoirs purport to reveal Henry IV's "Grand Design," is the next known writer to show Crucé's influence. Scholars now believe that this is Sully's own work and that he used Henry IV's name to honor the king he served and to lend authority to the plan. In the manuscript editions of Sully's work, which appeared before 1620, there is no mention of perpetual peace, but this topic suddenly receives full treatment in the edition of 1638, or, after Crucé. Pfister says: "This last concept . . . does not seem to us to be original. Sully took it, we think, from a very interesting and unusual book of the time, the Cinée d'Estat *written by an author who deserves to be remembered: Em: Lacroix."*[38] *Sully's solutions, as Grotius's, are less radical than Crucé's. It is thought that Sully took as his point of departure Henry's plan to reduce the power of the Houses of Spain and Austria but incorporated into it Crucé's higher ideal of a general peace. After achieving a balance of power in Europe, Henry was to have used this power against the Turks. Only after their subjugation could an era of universal peace begin.*

Later influences become increasingly difficult to demonstrate. Similar circumstances and a growing awareness of the need for cooperation among nations have brought both new thinkers and new statesmen to carry out ideas like Crucé's. "He [Crucé] has been repeated, but not surpassed."[39]

In the works of the Abbé de Saint-Pierre (of whom Leibnitz mentions Crucé as a precursor) many of the same ideas are found, but they came from Henry IV, through Sully from Crucé. Jean-Jacques Rousseau defended these ideas as they appeared in the Abbé de Saint-Pierre's writing. Jeremy Bentham and countless others have since supported them.

The Peace of Westphalia in 1648, the Congress of Vienna, the League of Nations, and the United Nations have attempted to follow at least modified versions of Crucé's plan, but their aim has always been to strengthen a certain position, never to attain total equilibrium, although each has been better than the last.[40]

Still, Crucé retains the honor of being "the first to have supported and the first to have drawn up an international organization that has been improved upon hardly at all since his time." [41]

In the field of economics, it is Louis-Lucas's opinion that Crucé goes far beyond the mercantilists and the physiocrats in his thinking. It is Adam Smith who most closely resembles him, and the two ideas for which Smith is most highly praised, namely a multiple basis for the economy and free-trade, are the two doctrines basic to Crucé's economic theory. [42]

Some of Crucé's ideas, as is only natural, are outmoded today. Uncivilized peoples are no longer compared to beasts, and neither are considered our natural enemies to be killed as an exercise for men of arms during peacetime (p. 26). We may note, however, that this notion was not changed until very recently, especially with respect to animals. It is also true that Crucé misjudged the real and potential value of some of the branches of knowledge. His casual acceptance of the divine right of kings and the primary position he would accord to the Papacy in a general assembly obviously reflect early seventeenth-century realities. And, while many of his criticisms of democracy are only too true, nevertheless he underestimated the profound effects that universal, free education, which he himself advocated, would have.

Still, when we consider the whole body of his thought, we are amazed to find the large number of his ideas that men have either already accepted, or are working to have accepted. His economic policies *have been adopted at least in part. The income tax is an integral part of finance; the promises that taxes can be reduced when war ceases are still heard; government loans are common; restrictions on the minting of money are no longer even discussed; problems brought about by the continual revaluation of currency are well known; the doctrine of completely free trade that was the culmination of Crucé's economic thinking is still a dream. There have been many approaches to it, meeting with varying degrees of success. Such efforts as the European Common Market would surely have Crucé's approval.*

In the realm of social welfare, too, many of Crucé's philosophies and suggestions have been accepted and implemented. Did he not recognize in the seventeenth century, the need for every honest man to have status in the community? Respect for the workingman has come only recently, and perhaps incompletely, although Crucé said, ". . . a prudent and gracious man never scorns anything he cannot do without" (p. 45). The idea of the census is firmly entrenched as is free public education, but the question of censorship is still much debated. Subsidies for the poor and the form they should take are subjects for a great deal of dissension, although the theory that the poor should be helped in some way is generally recognized. Other problems, too, are very modern in their concept: the right to control the police and the difficulties inherent in obtaining justice for all. Crucé advocates and finds historical precedent for the system of the public defender.

On his major points, of course, Crucé expresses the view of enlightened men of the twentieth century. That war is the greatest horror for mankind has been amply proved. That a small country, through alliances, can defeat a larger one and that countries of which we have never heard can suddenly rise and upset the world have been documented at length. Crucé warned in 1623 that it was folly to expect or try to force everyone to share one viewpoint, yet nations continue to try.

On the positive side, Crucé's greatest contribution, the concept of a permanent world association to settle disputes, has come ever closer to realization. The World Court at The Hague and the United Nations, while far from perfect, are enormous steps toward world peace.

Yet it is not Crucé's specific recommendations alone that allow us to call him a modern. It is also the enlightened philosophy that underlies them. He sees, for example, that evolution is inevitable; society is not static; but also that gradual changes make fewer enemies, and force makes no friends. As men in the twentieth century, he recognizes that open communication is the key to understanding. And, most remarkable, he perceives the theory of the relativity of values without which men cannot find a common ground for agreement.

What kind of man, then, was Eméric Crucé,

Parisien? *He was a visionary, but also a practical man. He was a scholar, but one who appreciated the work of the merchant, farmer, and artisan. He was a man bound by his time in some respects, but far in advance of it in others. He was a proud man, who believed his work worthy of the attention of kings, but one who had enough humility not to expect immediate results, since he closed his book by saying: "As for me, the only contribution I can make consists of wishes and humble expostulations, which will perhaps be useless. I nevertheless wanted to leave this witness to posterity. If it serves no purpose, have patience. It is a small thing to have wasted paper and words. . . . Some who will read this little book will be grateful to me and will honor me, I hope, with their remembrance" (p. 226). He was a man steeped in the history and traditions of the past, but whose efforts were bent toward improving the present and assuring the future. He was a man of intense feeling, capable of profound admiration and scathing scorn, whose concerns are as relevant today as they were in the seventeenth century.*

With the insights he has given us into his mind and heart, we need not regret the lack of details about his life. We know Eméric Crucé.

C. Frederick Farrell, Jr.
Edith R. Farrell
Morris, Minnesota

NOTES

[1] *For a discussion of some of these, see Pierre Louis-Lucas,* Un plan de paix générale *(Paris, 1919), pp. 2-5.*

[2] *"Histoire littéraire du droit international,"* Revue de droit international, *(XXII, 1890), p. 377.*

[3] *Nys,* op. cit. *Louis-Lucas,* op. cit. *Vesnitch, "Deux précurseurs français du pacifisme et de l'arbitrage international,"* Revue d'histoire diplomatique, *(1911), p. v.*

[4] *See Louis-Lucas, pp. 3-15, for a listing and commentary of the various references to Crucé from his own lifetime to the present.*

[5] *Em. Cr. Par.,* Le Nouveau Cynée ou Discours d'Estat. Représentant les occasions et moyens d'establir une paix générale, et la liberté du commerce par tout le monde. Aux Monarques et Princes Souverains de ce temps. *(Paris: Chez Jacques Villery, 1623), Avec Privilège du Roy, p. IX. (All references to Crucé are to the marginal numbers so that the reader may easily refer to this volume or to the French versions.)*

[6] *Louis-Lucas, p. 63.*

[7] *Louis-Lucas, p. 72.*

[8] *Vesnitch, p. 25.*

[9] *Vesnitch, pp. 25-34.*

[10] *Louis-Lucas, pp. 48-51.*

[11] *Louis-Lucas, p. 28.*

[12] *Louis-Lucas, p. 43.*

[13] *Louis-Lucas, pp. 52 ff.*

[14] *Louis-Lucas, p. 45.*

[15] *Cf. Louis-Lucas, pp. 28-48.*

[16] *Louis-Lucas, p. 48.*

[17] *Quoted in Nys, p. 383.*

[18]*Quoted in Louis-Lucas, p. 10.*

[19]*Quoted in Vesnitch, p. 63.*

[20]*See Nys, pp. 375-77, and Thomas W. Balch (trans. and ed.),* The New Cyneas of Eméric Crucé *(Philadelphia, 1909), pp. v-vi.*

[21]*(Paris: 1751?-1765 [Dates verified in the Library of Congress Catalogue of Printed Cards].) Quoted in Nys, p. 383.*

[22]*P. 186.*

[23]Ibid., *p. 187.*

[24]*Quoted in Balch, p. xxv (footnote).*

[25]*Anonymous, "Art. X. The Question of Arbitration in the House of Commons; being the Substance of the Debate on Mr. Cobden's Motion in favour of Arbitration Treaties instead of War, for the settlement of International Disputes. With an Appendix." (London: Charles Gilpin) XXVI, 241.*

[26]*Quoted in Vesnitch, p. 75.*

[27]*Nys, p. 378.*

[28]*Balch, p. xxviii.*

[29]*"Le Nouveau Cinée Émeric Crucée,"* Revue de droit international et de législation comparée, *(1910) p. 42.*

[30]*Vesnitch, pp. 77-78.*

[31]*Louis-Lucas, p. 185.*

[32]*Louis-Lucas, p. 125.*

[33]Studies in Statecraft *(Cambridge), p. 100.*

[34]*Cf. Louis-Lucas, pp. 19 ff.*

[35]*Louis-Lucas, pp. 17 and 19.*

[36]*Due to the limitations of an introduction, a detailed analysis of the genesis of the various subjects treated by Crucé is not possible here. The reader is referred to the relevant chapters in Louis-Lucas's thesis for further study.*

[37]*Louis-Lucas, pp. 153-54.*

[38]*Quoted in Louis-Lucas, p. 157.*

[39]*Louis-Lucas, p. 164.*

[40]*Cf. Louis-Lucas, pp. 171 ff.*

NOTES

[41] *Louis-Lucas, p. 179.*

[42] *Louis-Lucas, p. 135.*

BIBLIOGRAPHY OF WORKS CITED IN THE INTRODUCTION

Balch, Thomas Willing (trans. and ed.). The New Cyneas of Eméric Crucé. *Philadelphia: Allen, Lane and Scott, 1909.*

Butler, Sir Geoffrey Gilbert. Studies in Statecraft. Being Chapters Biographical and Bibliographical on the Sixteenth Century. *Cambridge: The University Press, 1920.*

Crucé, Eméric. Le Nouveau Cynée ou Discours d'Estat. Représentant les occasions et moyens d'establir une paix générale, et la liberté du commerce par tout le monde. Aux Monarques et Princes Souverains de ce temps. *Paris: Chez Jacques Villery, 1623. Avec Privilège du Roy.*

Louis-Lucas, Pierre. Un Plan de paix générale et de liberté du commerce au XVIIe siècle: Le Nouveau Cynée d'Eméric Crucé (1623). *Paris: L. Tenin, 1919.*

PERIODICALS

Crick, Daniel, "Le Noveau Cynée d'Émeric Crucé," Revue de droit international et de législation comparée *(1910), 35-50.*

Nys, Ernest. "Histoire littéraire du droit international. – A Propos de la paix perpétuelle de l'Abbé de Saint-Pierre. Eméric Crucé et Ernest, Landgrave de Hesse-Rheinfels," Revue de droit international et de législation comparée, *XXII (1890), 371-384.*

"The Question of Arbitration in the House of Commons; being

the Substance of the Debate on Mr. Cobden's Motion in favour of Arbitration Treaties instead of War, for the settlement of International Disputes. With an Appendix. London: Charles Gilpin," Eclectic Review, *XXVI (August, 1849), 236-251.*

"Utopistes Célèbres," Magasin Pittoresque *(1839), 186-187.*

Vesnitch, M[ilan R.] "Deux précurseurs français du pacifisme et de l'arbitrage international," Revue d'histoire diplomatique *(1911), 23-78.*

A Note on the Translation

There exist two editions of The New Cineas *in the* Bibliothèque Nationale *in Paris. One is dated 1623; the other 1624. M. Roger Pierrot, Head Curator of the* Département des Imprimés *of the* Bibliothèque Nationale *and M. J. Chazelas, Secretary of the* Académie des Sciences Morales et Politiques *of the French Institute have both verified that these two editions are identical with the exception of the title page. The 1624 edition has a new, shorter title affixed to the original (see Bibliography).*

The Harvard Library acquired a copy of this work, but with the title page missing, from the collection of Charles Sumner. It was from this source that Thomas W. Balch made the copy that he published in 1909 together with his own English translation.

The marginal numbers in the present volume correspond to the original page numbers of the Harvard copy. They are also found in the Balch edition, which is more readily available. It is to these numbers that the Index refers.

Unfortunately there are a number of errors in the Balch copy. They range from omitted words to misspellings that change one word to another. Such errors obscure the meaning of the text.

The present translation is based not on the French

of Balch's edition, but on that of the Harvard copy. Scholars who have only the Balch edition for a comparison of the English and French and who find discrepancies will know that it was in those places that errors occurred.

Mr. Balch, although not a French scholar, made a very real contribution. Through his work, Crucé's theories were made available to the English-speaking world. His edition also allowed such collections as the Library of Congress and the British Museum to acquire copies of a French version that they would not otherwise have had. It is neither necessary nor desirable to point out the errors in his English text. Some were a result of the miscopying of the French; others occurred through a misinterpretation of false cognates or lack of verification of proper nouns.

Nevertheless, since a new English edition was to be printed, it seemed appropriate to have a new translation. The errors in text and translation mentioned above were an important factor in this decision. There was still another. Mr. Balch stated as his aim "to render rather the author's meaning than to give a smooth English style." The result was a translation that may have been somewhat difficult to read in 1909. Parts of it are almost unintelligible in 1972.

Our goal has been different. We have attempted to retain the flavor of the seventeenth century, but to strive above all for clarity. For this reason, we have divided long sentences and paragraphs, modernized the wording, and used the present-day version of proper nouns.

The result, we hope, is a more readable English text, which still conveys Crucé's thought and which may be checked against the original editions by using the marginal numbers.

The New Cineas

Preface

This book could be sent throughout the inhabited world and offered to all kings for their inspection without fear of incurring disgrace, for it has been guided by truth, and the importance of its subject matter may well serve in place of letters of recommendation and credit. The author is quite unlike Dinocrates, the engineer, whose designs and bas-reliefs were beautiful but impractical. On the contrary, he expresses the wishes and desires of all men of good will and offers helpful advice, the execution of which depends on those
who hold the key to world affairs. He does not attempt II
to accuse anyone, still less to flatter. No one can say that he has strayed from the path of truth out of love either for his country or his religion, even though these loves are so engraved on his soul that death itself cannot efface them. The author's aim is not to settle controversies, nor is it to deliver eulogies or condemnations. He leaves such speechmaking to the theologians and orators and encourages them to make use of their eloquence and golden pen in so noble and important a cause. Some men excel in explaining the mysteries of religion, and in proving them to non-believers by quoting irreproachable authorities. This is fine, but our first task must be to uproot inhumanity, the most rampant of all vices and the source of all the others.

Not every age and place has been plagued by heresy.

III And atheism is even rarer. There is no man so brutish or so unreasonable that he can look up at the heavens and deny the existence of a divine power. We do see countless men today who do not feel obliged to believe anything but what reason reveals to them. Thus, although they recognize a divine power, they cannot subscribe to the other articles of the creed, because they are not enlightened on this subject by that natural light of reason which must, according to their views, govern all beliefs and all opinions and yet not be bound by them. However, they would not dare assert this publicly. Outwardly they conform to the beliefs and customs of their country for fear of being denounced as atheists, even though they really are not. It would be more appropriate to call them agnostics, particularly since they follow only the dictates of reason and scorn theological faith as if they believed it to be only an imaginary virtue.

The number of such men grows each day, for neither
IV the written nor the spoken word is any longer accepted uncritically. Assertions accepted as undeniable in youth suddenly come under suspicion when men can think them through and reflect upon the oracular pronouncement of the Royal Prophet: *Every man is capable of lying.*

This is why the most renowned preachers, recognizing that a doctrine so far removed from common sense can have little effect on the minds of men today, concentrate their efforts on trying to improve morals. This is the most effective way of making people well-disposed toward piety. Piety takes a firmer hold in the mind of a good man than it does in that of an evil

man, for the latter's belief in God is sustained only through habit. Can a slanderer, a deceitful man, or a murderer be judged in any other way? Is it likely that
these men believe in Hell, or the immortality of the V
soul? No matter what preachers do, they will never persuade them otherwise; they will only give outsiders grounds for doubting the worth of Christian beliefs.

In the time of Saint Louis, the Tartars had decided to embrace Christianity, but they were dissuaded when they heard about the terrible things that the Christians were doing. Whether or not they had a valid point will not be broached here. The fact remains that integrity and morality are essential to the survival of religion. This fact must be preached to the great and the humble, to Kings and their subjects, instead of wasting time on scholastic disputes that produce a great deal more noise than positive results. I know that heresies must be refuted, but I see none greater than the error made by those who place injustice above all else and who value only arms.

Can we hope to see any improvement in religion or VI
any peace in the state as long as this reprehensible opinion is accepted? Yet this belief is allowed to insinuate itself into the minds of the people; no one mentions it, any more than they would an unimportant subject. On the contrary, by remaining silent men seem to lend tacit consent to it. This is what prompted me to make public this reminder and plan for peace which the reader will find new by virtue of its format and the extent of its subject matter.

Peace is a common topic of conversation, I admit, but its realization is sought only through halfway measures.

Some urge Christian rulers to band together for mutual protection against their common enemy. A famous person has even shown ways of exterminating the Turks
VII in four years or so and has written about other lovely plans which are very easy to accomplish – on paper.

There are others, more modest, who invent means of organizing and enriching their own countries and demonstrate so little concern for other nations that they feel it is only prudent politics to seek to divide these nations in order to enjoy a more secure peace themselves. But I am of quite different opinion. It seems to me that when a man sees his neighbor's house burning or falling down, he has good reason to be fearful as well as compassionate, considering that human society is one body whose members are so closely related to one another that misfortunes which attack one will necessarily spread to the others.

Now, this little book contains a universal policy which can be used by all nations alike and will be acceptable to anyone having any spark of reason and humanitarian feeling. As for the others, I predict that
VIII they will not read this work, or if they do, they will not pay any attention to it. Among these are certainly those ambitious warriors, who scornfully refer to us as "men who live in an ivory tower," and in order to shame us quote that old proverb which says "Those who can, do; those who can't, teach." I freely grant them this, provided that what they do is good and not evil. There was a time when I would have answered these men of action otherwise. Now they will have to be content with this: I am not writing for the barbarians and ignoramuses who will be scandalized by this work. Nor

will what I have written appeal to those who lack sufficient insight and therefore will perhaps compare it to Plato's *Republic* which was never anything more than an idea in the imagination of its author. This comparison, however, would not be valid, for what we are proposing here is not only possible, but it is IX
something that was tried in ancient times.

In the time of Caesar Augustus, all nations lived in peace, and during the reign of Francis I peace flourished for a few years throughout all Europe. Who is preventing us from hoping for something that was known to be good in centuries past? I believe that there is nothing easier than bringing about peace, if Christian rulers, and especially our French Hercules, Louis the Just, whose surname seems to me to be a good omen, want to make the effort. It must not be said, therefore, that proposals for universal peace are illusionary or ill-founded. Everyone will judge this book as he wishes. I hope that it will find a place in the library of great men and that judicious persons will take it into account however they may be inclined.

THE NEW CINEAS

or

Discourse on Opportunities and Means for Establishing a General Peace and Freedom of Trade Throughout the World

To the monarchs and sovereign rulers of our time.

I had no intention of addressing this treatise to the common man, who is dependent on a master and whose actions are guided by no established set of rules. I felt it even less desirable to address my remarks to men of violence who disregard all rules of honesty and who
respect nothing except force. It is you, the great men, 2
who will, I hope, receive this little book favorably; it is in your hands, *High*, *Powerful*, and *Invincible Monarchs*, that I place it.

It is certainly not that I think you need any additional advice, for when God placed you in such an exalted position, He bestowed virtue upon you in proportion to the demands of your office. But since advice which comes from an honest man who has never been suspected of doing evil is generally well-received, and since a fortune, however great, is subject to change, I thought it would not be inappropriate to show you, in all humility, ways by which you could make your state secure through the establishment of universal peace.

Even if this matter did not involve you personally, the public interest alone would certainly be sufficient to persuade you to have pity on the human race, which calls upon you with one voice for peace and begs you, for your own sakes, to end its sufferings and to put a stop to the abuses which the horrors of war have produced up to now. This request is only politic. It is much more reasonable to heed these arguments than the

3 unbridled passions of those warriors who, like the ancient Persians, can envision only battles and victories. Such men deck themselves out in their cursed uniforms and glorify injustice and oppression above all else. I shall not waste my time declaiming against such men who are, by nature, grossly perverted.

It will suffice to mention the causes of war. Once these causes are known, one can only deplore the blindness that permits men to treat others with so much cruelty for such frivolous reasons. But before I begin, I wish to state that I do not intend these words to apply to civil wars and uprisings. So treacherous men need not think that they can use this treatise as a justification for their revolts. Neither should they lay claim to a right to peace which they do not deserve if they do not recognize their sovereign and renounce their factions.

Setting aside, then, mutinies, of which I shall speak later, I contend that foreign wars are undertaken for honor, for profit, for righting some wrong, or for
4 exercise. Religion might be added if experience did not show that this usually serves as a mere pretext. I have also left out necessity which in the past has forced a number of people to leave their homes *en masse* and to go and take possession of new ones by force. This is why colonies are so frequently mentioned in history. Today, however, these waves of homeless people are rare. So much so, that we cannot find any motives or causes for war other than the four mentioned above, of which the first is the most common and seems to be the most legitimate.

If the desire for honor is natural to a noble man, then it is certainly fitting that he seek it through the exercise

of arms, on which all glory depends. At least this is the consensus of public opinion, which it would be folly to contradict. All nations agree on this matter, and ancient as well as modern customs have always given soldiers the privileges of nobility and command. Since this is so, the honors accorded to all other kinds of virtue and ability pale when compared to military prowess. Most rulers, accepting this error as truth, place value on nothing but 5
arms.

This unfortunate belief is not of recent origin. The Emperor Severus commanded his children to give rich rewards to soldiers and to scorn all other men. And Pyrrhus, the king of Albania, when asked to whom he would leave his kingdom, answered "To whoever has the best sword." But these words smack of barbarism and brutality. To them we might oppose the authority of the good Lacedemonian king who felt that justice was better than valor and who said that the latter was in no way necessary when reason and integrity held sway. In fact, why should so much value be placed on something that the most stupid animal can do?

Hurting and killing are easy. A little asp, a single fly can accomplish it. That ought to be enough to humble those bullies who boast of having killed so many men in various skirmishes and battles. It is an honorable thing, they say, to defeat one's enemy. Do we have any 6
enemies other than wild beasts? There is a kind of friendship and kinship among men that springs from the basic similarity in their nature and physical appearance. Everyone likes to have a portrait of himself and takes pleasure in this inanimate reproduction of his features. But we show less respect for our living images; we pride

ourselves on ruining our fellow man, while at the same time ignominiously fleeing the field of battle on which we should engage our natural enemies: lions, tigers, wolves, and snakes.

We no longer dare either stalk or attack these beasts except by trickery, just as those who know themselves to be weak use ruses and strategems to surprise their adversaries. Now, if these animals had any intelligence among them, they could dispose of man in very little time. The hot wind, at one time, depopulated certain regions of Africa; an overabundance of snakes ruined a city; and a scourge of rats and frogs has caused whole nations to flee their lands.

7 How do we know that God will not, once again, use such means to punish our iniquities? In fact, there is little cause to flourish our swords, since it takes so little to lay us low. We have good cause to brag about our strength when animals have such a great advantage over us in this respect that we can say that this is the least perfect of human attributes.

Consequently, ordinary valor, having no other foundation or support but brute force, is not really worth praising. I say "ordinary valor" to distinguish it from magnanimity which is characterized by steadfastness of courage and scorn for all adversities. These are the marks of true valor: to reject all wrongs and to do none; to suffer death and all other misfortunes nobly when they occur, but not to go seeking them in the hope of finding some ill-defined honor.

The futility of such honor has been recognized at the last moment even by those who prized it all their lives.

Do we not see, when these people are dying, how they regret having abandoned themselves to the changing
dictates of such a foolish notion? Then they solemnly 8
renounce and repent. I have even seen some who, when mortally wounded, swore that they would take the habit and spend the rest of their days in devotions should they recover. It is logical to assume that those who die in battle have similar thoughts.

Reason knocks continuously at our doors and whispers incessantly in our ears. The time to heed it is not when we are about to leave this world. In such cases, we see the unfortunate plight of those who recognize their errors only when they are *in extremis*, and who adopt a reasonable point of view only when they are no longer capable of doing wrong. They are swayed by public opinion, ruled by custom, and blinded by ambition. As a result, they trample on all forms of respect, caring neither for God nor men; their only concern is making everyone talk about them. But in this they are sometimes badly mistaken, for instead of acquiring the reputation they desire and dying in an honorable bed, they fall into the basest kind of servitude and are used as playthings by their enemies.

Imagine the situation of prisoners of war: the insults 9
and scorn that would be unbearable for any ordinary citizen, and in the end, the hangman's noose or some other painful and ignominious death. Yet these are the usual results of war. Every soldier, gentleman, captain, and commander is subject to this plight. The greatest of kings and emperors are not exempt. Valerian, Baldwin, Tomabais, Bajazet, Atahualpa, and others who ended their days ignominiously have provided a valuable lesson

for all rulers. That is, there is more dishonor to be feared than honor to be gained in war. For evil comes about more often than good, and if it is true that it is folly to leave the certain for the uncertain, then rulers should protect their honor. They should not risk it in order to satisfy the appetites and urgings of those who hold out hope and who mention what they might be able to gain and not what they might lose. These persons outline future conquests, make the rulers imagine triumphal arches, but do not show them the ignominious yoke under which they will be in danger of passing. These men quote over and over the old maxim: "The monarchy is a beautiful sepulchre: it is well worth taking a risk for it."

This would be all well and good to say to ambitious and desperate individuals who would be willing to risk their lives in an attempt to attain greatness. But rulers who have already acquired power and authority should not expose themselves to the unpredictable ways of fortune which plays with the greatest of men and produces unforeseen setbacks in the greatest of enterprises.

At present, world affairs are in such a state that there is no dukedom so small that it cannot, by means of alliances, resist the most powerful king on earth. A wise prince, therefore, will not launch out against another state for fear of wrecking his own. Even though ambition might move him to risk his own life and that of his subjects, let him at least take thought for his honor, about which he shows so much concern. Let him consider carefully the shame and the injury which come to warmongers. They put themselves on the very brink

of ruin. The slightest upset can hurl them down into the
abyss of misery. When at the height of their prosperity, 11
they think they have attained heaven on earth, a reversal of fate will suddenly tumble them, and other sovereigns will make them slaves. There they are, captives in chains with the executioner at their heels. Then they see how far removed they are from the glory they had pictured for themselves; they have an abundance of leisure time in which to bewail the happiness which they could have enjoyed in peace had they not had such unlimited ambitions.

These are not unfounded ideas that we have thought up. History testifies and experience verifies that war more often weakens than enhances the reputation of a ruler. Even though a ruler might acquire as much glory as Caesar ever had, or if he could have the universe as his empire if he won, would it not still be cruel to arrive at his goal by such vile means?

Oh what a wretched thing honor is if it must be bought with such an outpouring of blood! I venerate
your memory, Otho Salvius, pride of your century, sole 12
hope and delight of those Roman soldiers who voluntarily sacrificed their fortunes and their lives to raise you to the imperial throne and gave you their arms as a guarantee of their loyalty and affection. You refused their offer, preferring to die as a simple gentleman rather than to acquire a kingdom at the cost of so many faithful servants' lives. This one act is worth all the empires in the world. Posterity will prefer it to all the laurels of the Caesars, for many have imitated them, but your noble goodness remains forever unequaled.

Must monarchs gain their positions by massacres and

butchery? Certainly not. They are not thieves that they must proceed in this fashion. They are images of God, guardians of their people, destined to heal and not to wound, to build and not to destroy.

But even if we were to concede that war was necessary to found monarchies, there is no longer any need today, when they are already established, for those who enjoy them to fill the world with carnage. Why do monarchs need to set out on campaigns? Without striking a single blow, they already have the honor of sovereign command, which is the very thing they seek
13 with so much difficulty and apparently with so little chance of success. Let them remain on the defensive. Preserving a kingdom is difficult enough. Let them keep firmly in mind that they run a great risk of losing their honor in war and that any gain is uncertain. For every two soldiers who become rich, there are fifty who will get only wounds or incurable illnesses as a result of war.

As for rulers, they ruin their treasuries waging it. Philip II of Spain would have something to say about this. He spent millions in gold to so little advantage that he served as an example to his successor to make a useful search for peace in those places where he might have waged a useless war. The one who could boast about his military exploits the most is the Sultan. Besides, his ventures have succeeded so well that there is no monarchy at this time that can compare with his. Nevertheless, look at what he has gained in the last few years. He has done almost nothing but hold his own and has been reduced to extremities by his own subjects,
14 who have forced him to think of his own self-preservation rather than new conquests. They have

made him realize that if force establishes monarchies, it also ruins them, even though they seem to have attained all the power and glory that is humanly possible. On the other hand, the Christians have not made any greater progress in their affairs. They have the misfortune, should they win some victory, not to be able to enjoy it for long, while the Turks on the contrary have stability and are not easily dispossessed of what they own.

I am contrasting these two peoples because they are, in a way, natural enemies and have divided almost the whole world into two parts because of the differences between their religions. If they could come to an agreement, it would be a great step forward in the cause of universal peace. For a Christian ruler, seeing himself at peace with the Mohamedan, would be even more eager to come to an agreement with another member of his own religion, and the Sultan, being in agreement with the Christians, would be more amenable in his dealings with the king of Persia or Tartary. As for the pagans and the Jews, I do not think that they would refuse to be included in so general a treaty, and if they did, their best efforts would not be enough to prevent its good effects. The whole difficulty lies in the claims of a few sovereigns who have been deprived of all or part of their domains.

Herein lies the third reason for war: when rulers take up arms in order to recover their former rights and to avenge the wrong done them. But anyone who examines the origins of empires and kingdoms will conclude for himself that these claims are ill-founded. For monarchies are not acquired in the same way as other inheritances. They come directly from God and are

established by His providence alone. He gives scepters and takes them away at will and, at the same time, deprives kings of the means for recovering them. There are many who can testify to this, particularly the Holy Roman Emperor. Who has a more just cause for complaint than he, given that most modern kingdoms
16 are built on the ruins of his state? Nevertheless, he is forced to be satisfied with the little that he still has and to remember that, as his Empire at one time grew and became rich on the spoils of the world, it finally had to serve as prey to other nations, each of which carried off considerable portions of it. No mention need be made of other rulers who vainly struggled to recover what they had lost and in so doing discovered that, in this, kingdoms are like men: they are born, they mature, and they decline.

We must not flatter ourselves by saying that God favors just causes. That is to presume too intimate an understanding of His providence and to reassure ourselves that He will favor us rather than another. The expectation of this imagined favor has caused many who presumed themselves in the right to undertake wars, thinking that God would use them as an instrument to exterminate some power which they themselves thought to be unjust and tyrannical. They found that they were far from justified in their calculations, and for every league that they expected to gain from the usurpers, they lost fifty, besides putting their whole state in
17 danger. Some have even lost their lives and honor in such ventures.

It is right for a ruler to oppose courageously anyone who seeks to encroach upon his country. But when he has been completely deprived of it, and because of his impotence cannot re-establish himself, then he must surrender, not perhaps to men but to God. God is jealous of kingdoms, which are His most beautiful works, and on them He has engraven the image of His majesty, the marks of His virtue. He declares Himself their protector by visible signs, particularly when they have been fortified by long possession. Those who attack them will fare no better than did the Ancients who tried to cut the Isthmus of Corinth.

It is not within the power of men to disrupt a divinely established order, such as monarchies. Rulers who are involved in such matters, either through the total ruin of their state or through the diminution of the same, must remember that God is by no means obligated to continue to give His blessing to any one place. If He transferred their scepter to another's hand, He had done the same favor for their predecessors
whom He created out of dust, giving them absolute 18
power to enjoy their possessions so long as it pleased Him and no longer. Rulers should not complain, therefore, about an evil common to all estates. They should not call usurpation what time, fortune, and God's will has authorized. Let them restrain their vain hopes and the desire for a vengeance that they cannot take. Even if it could be carried out, they should try some other means, and before resorting to arms, they should submit to arbitration by sovereign potentates and lords. By doing this, they would gain the friendship of their peers which could be used against their enemies in case the latter did not wish to abide by the decision of a third party. Now if a ruler found that his case were

to be judged by someone who arrogantly tried to meddle in arranging the differences, then this situation would indeed detract from his grandeur. The voluntary acceptance of arbitrators, however, is something that was done in former times and is still done by monarchs.

If it is possible to terminate amicably quarrels resulting from the desire to acquire possession of sovereign principalities, then it will be easier to settle
19 peaceably other disputes and differences of opinion
which arise among great men, concerning their boundaries, allowances, tributes, and other rights of lesser importance. And this would apply as well to offensive actions or words which often precipitate cruel wars for lack of a third party capable of reconciling the differences in a way satisfactory to the offended party. The general assembly, about which we shall speak later, would be of great assistance in this type of situation. Thus, the third cause of war can be refuted.

There remains the fourth which, I admit, is more difficult to remedy, given that men, and particularly soldiers, are naturally restless. That is why we read of so many peoples who, in former times, went into exile, voluntarily leaving their own countries to seek war elsewhere. They were not able to stand the thought that their arms should become weak while their generosity grew strong. This same consideration forced some kings to release their subjects and allow them to go to try their fortunes elsewhere. These rulers feared that their subjects might imitate those ancient Odrysians who
20 slashed their own bodies with swords when they could
find no more enemies to conquer. The Germans, with this same goal in mind, trained their young men to be

highway robbers to give them a pastime.

A fine speech-maker who prefers to remain anonymous asks: How will all our valiant men, who can smell only gunpowder, whose hand is at home only on the hilt of a sword, and whose foot is at home only on a battlefield or the breach of a wall, spend their time? The answer to this question is very brief. The world is not made for the sort of man who can do nothing but evil. They do not belong in the court of kings. They should all be sent to live with the Cannibals and the Savages whose only human trait is their face. It is an unnatural man who seeks repose in disturbance, honor in infamy, and a pastime in inhumanity.

Suppress (great monarchs) suppress these men of monstruous courage, these frenzied souls who follow, not princes, but their fortunes, who abandon them when it is convenient, and who often betray them. What can be expected of men who thrive on blood and carnage? Undoubtedly a ruler needs soldiers for his own 21
protection and for that of the state, but when he has weighed the good and the evil that may come of them, he will see that it is much more dangerous to exalt them than to humble them. A warrior's heart is ambitious and violent and pays no attention to what it has, only to what it can get.

Can we not find many examples of this in the last century and in our own? The Roman Emperors found themselves in serious difficulty because they gave in to the soldiers of the palace guard. The mutineers gave away, or to be more exact, sold the empire, disposing of it as they saw fit. Hardly had they sworn allegiance to their master when they were already dissatisfied and

killed him cruelly and put another in his place. The new ruler was accepted under the same conditions as the former, that is, he ran the risk of undergoing a similar fate whenever it seemed good to those executioners to pass the sentence of death on him to whom they
22 submitted their lives. Thus the Sultan often takes orders from those who call themselves his slaves.

What a pitiful sight to see a sovereign forced to give up his most faithful servants to the will of mutinous troops, who present their request with weapons in hand and boldly threaten their prince as though he owed his imperial crown to them. This is what will be the downfall of the Ottomans; their Empire will never be destroyed except by the excessive power that they have given and still give the Janissaries. Now if they were willing to listen to counsel for peace and seek public tranquility along with other monarchs, they would not put up with these blusterers. They would be better served and would be in no way dependent on the caprices of unruly men to whom they always have to make concessions. The emperor Probus, taking this into consideration, said flatly that he would arrange affairs in such a way that soldiers would not be needed.

Great Princes, it is within your power to carry out
23 this holy resolution. The human race, and particularly your own people, will be grateful to you. There is no conquest worth such great acclaim; there is no victory more deserving of a joyful celebration. What greater honor can you desire than to see peace proclaimed throughout the world during your reign? Historians will record your name in letters of gold; men will speak of your reign as the beginning or the return of the Golden

Age. No longer will they speak of the conquests of Alexander, or the triumphs of Caesar, or the stratagems of Hannibal and Sertorius. The vanity of those warriors, who gloried in murder and pillage instead of feeling eternal remorse and shame, will finally be recognized. Instead, posterity will take as its heroes those brave men who, having overcome the monsters of inhumanity and barbarity, will regulate the universe according to the laws of justice, in short, those who show themselves to be true images of the divine.

Now a good name cannot be acquired by pillagings, massacres, or other hostile acts, but only by a compassionate government, a legitimate and controlled power. This is what distinguishes kingdoms from robber 24
bands and tyrannies, which are full of anxieties and do not last. The greatness of a King must not be judged by the extent of his power. Agesilaus became angry because the King of Persia was called "great." How can he be greater than I, he asked, unless he be more just? The true greatness of a Sovereign lies in the prompt obedience given him by his subjects and in the undisturbed enjoyment of his estate. These things cannot come about so long as he is engaged in war, for war brings with it a great change in attitudes and makes the people less obedient and respectful. Such a sovereign, who in time of war is forced to court his vassal and to woo the lowest soldier with fair promises, rules with the rod even in time of peace.

And what is the object of all these shameful submissions? To be able to trample upon one's neighbor, to make oneself feared. If your courage is so great that it beckons you to a more exalted station, if

you cannot be satisfied with your present possessions, at
25 least follow the example of the eagles who, by tacit consent, designate a certain part of the sky in which each will seek its prey, and none goes out of these boundaries. Limit your territory as the wise Numa did, and, following his advice, offer bloodless sacrifice to the God Terminus. Augustus took this attitude and voluntarily limited the extent of his Empire and, by the same token, his desires. He gave a good example of how to make use of warriors. After he had established peace, he put strong garrisons on his frontiers. In addition, he had two well-equipped and well-staffed fleets on the seas that could be called upon when needed.

This should satisfy those who say that valor would degenerate if a general peace were to be established. I could answer that if the whole world were at peace, there would be no reason for becoming seasoned to war, and that it is better to be a coward than a brute and a barbarian. The Romans anticipated these difficulties and took precautions so as not to become cowardly in peacetime. They got exercise in tournaments, fired at
26 the quintain, staged mock battles both on land and at sea in order to prepare themselves for serious encounters, and especially to avoid the boredom inherent in a long period of idleness. Every man grows stale if he does not work at his trade. That is why a soldier, whose only talent is his knowledge of fighting, should be given a target against which he can limber up his arm and measure his strength and dexterity honorably without commiting murder.

Since those who like something enjoy seeing it dramatized, those who want combat are happy to see a mock battle. And if they do not like such games, if they want to fight in earnest, then wild beasts will serve as suitable opponents for working off this desire for violence. Hunting is a noble and fitting exercise for warriors, especially for those skilled at it. I include among beasts, savages who do not use reason. These savages are good targets for war, as are pirates and thieves who do nothing but steal.

These are occasions where soldiers have a legitimate
purpose. They will have no cause for complaint, since 27
they will still be necessary for maintaining peace and for
keeping in power rulers who cannot feel secure without
arms. Rulers, therefore, should not scorn those who
make arms their profession but should grant them
certain privileges and even a decent livelihood so as to
remove all cause for discontent.

If the state of their finances be such that rulers
cannot be this liberal, then they have two recourses
open to them. First, they can dismiss some of their
warriors and retain only the most robust and the most
suitable, as did Julius Caesar. He limited the excessive
number of citizens living at the expense of the Republic
and reduced the army to 150,000 men. The other
remedy is to levy a special tax for the maintenance of a
police force to which everyone would be happy to
contribute, even though it might be somewhat
inconvenient, in order to be sure of having peace and of
avoiding the oppression and outrages suffered at the 28
hands of poorly paid soldiers.

One of the primary benefits of peace is to be able to control the behavior of the police, but it is impossible as long as they are either not paid at all or put off too long with promises. It is not enough, however, merely to hold such persons in check and to prevent their becoming restless as a result of too much leisure. Townspeople, who are no easier to govern, must be watched too. Villagers are for the most part too busy to think of anything but their own households. In a city one finds many penniless idlers. Not knowing what else to do, they look for trouble. Rome was greatly disturbed by such rabble. It existed on graft alone and blithely aided and abetted traitorous magistrates in pillaging, massacring, and sowing confusion.

To eliminate this evil, we need to revive the ancient custom of the Athenians and Egyptians. Among these people everyone had to give an account of his life, and those who had done nothing were punished. The Chinese do not put up with drones either, recognizing
29 that they provide a breeding ground for thieves, assassins, and factionists. Prince Hipparchus became angry when he saw an idle man. He exhorted the idler to work, and, so that there would be no excuse for not doing so, he offered him land and oxen with which to work it.

Agriculture and trade are two necessary occupations that are no less honorable than anything else. A man's work, courage, industry, and foresight are clearly seen in both. Agriculture nourishes a state; trade enlarges it. It is wrong to think that these trades are uninventive or degrading to the nobility. Roman gentlemen put their own hand to the plow and maintained stewards in various provinces through whose agency they were able to keep up trade. Even today there are rulers who have ships at sea which they send to foreign countries and

from which they realize a large profit. It is certainly
wrong to downgrade the merchant, especially one who,
with noble resolve, undertakes hazardous voyages in
order to enrich both himself and his country. He cannot 30
do the one without the other, and since the public is
composed of individuals, it reflects the wealth or the
poverty of the latter. It is not the great number of
priests, ministers, and monks who bring commodities to
a kingdom, even though they have great dignity and are
necessary to guarantee heaven's favor. Nor is it the
practitioners and officers of justice, who should not be
so numerous as they are in some places. In short, there
is no line of work as useful as commerce. The merchant
has every right to increase his wealth in return for his
work which is often done at the risk of his own life, but
without injuring or offending anyone else. In this
respect he deserves more credit than the soldier who is
promoted solely in proportion to his ability to despoil
and ruin others.

Since we are here dealing with the problem of
banishing idleness and turning to better use the evil
thoughts to which it usually gives rise in the minds of
good-for-nothings, there is no better expedient than
commerce. Therefore, a ruler ought to offer his subjects 31
all kinds of inducements to encourage them to take it
up as a profession. And as Cyrus, who wanted to debase
his Lydian rebels, subtly suggested that they frequent
theaters, brothels, and cabarets, so, if you wish to make
a people active and hard-working, you must open ships
and invite everyone, the great and the humble, to trade.
Neither of these groups will be willing to give themselves
to this project as long as they see the merchants so

disparaged and, what is worse, subject to so many restrictions.

It is only right that the ruler realize some small profit on the goods imported and exported to and from his country. But he should, as far as possible, exercise moderation, especially when necessary products such as wheat, wine, salt, fish, wool, linen, and hides are involved. If he does this, then the merchants will be able to trade more freely, and the people will be able to buy at a lower price. This will make them more contented, and instead of murmuring against their ruler, they will revere him as they would a propitious star or an earthly God. They will bless him and give a thousand testimonials to his good will. If this be the case, he will
32 not need soldiers, since he will be in firm control within his kingdom.

Once we have attained universal peace which will permit the establishment of commerce, the ruler will protect himself against foreign countries through the maintenance of a few companies of militia even if they are not often required. They will also serve to reassure those people who do not feel secure without them. Monarchs must see to it that their subjects may conduct their business both on land and on the seas without fear. Each can easily do this for his own particular realm.

In order to get a good start, care must be taken to assure that not only the large rivers but also the small ones are navigable, since the ease with which commerce is carried out depends on this. Those who have no rivers must get waterways by mechanical means as the Brabantines did when they built a canal from Brussels to
33 the Scheldt River so as to have better communications

with Antwerp. There are enough good rivers in France, but they only flood neighboring fields and estates. This was demonstrated in the council of King Charles IX who had resolved to take care of the matter, but troubles arose and disrupted the plans. For some time now it has been proposed that several navigable rivers be joined. The effort and money for this project would certainly be well-spent.

If one considers commerce in general, however, it would be more profitable to join two seas. This can be done in only three ways, which have, up to now, been practiced with more enthusiasm than positive results. These three ways are by cutting a strait between two seas, by cutting a canal from a river that flows into one sea and is located not far from the other, or by joining with a trench two rivers each of which flows into a different sea.

The first method was practiced by King Demetrius and the Emperors Julian, Caligula, and Nero, who tried to cut the Isthmus of Corinth which separates the Aegean Sea from the Ionian, but they were not
successful. The second was used by Ptolemy who dug a 34
canal between the Nile and the Red Sea, but he did not follow through on the project because he was informed that the sea lay higher than Egypt and would consequently flood the entire country. After a lapse of several centuries, the Sultans and the Turks had the same idea while trying to find an easier route to the Indies.

Charlemagne met with more success with the last method, that is, joining two seas. He joined the Altmuhl and the Regnitz in Franconia. The first flows into the

Danube and from there into the Mediterranean Sea. The other joins the Main and the Rhine and finally flows into the North Sea.

By joining the two seas, many of the detours that must be made and numerous hazards and inconveniences that are encountered in traveling from one sea to the other were to be avoided. While this work was in progress, the rainfall was so heavy that the ditches were filled with mire. It would be easy to finish this worthy project if only there were peace in Germany. There is another place where these two seas could be joined. It is in Languedoc, where a trench could be constructed from the Aude, which flows through Narbonne into the Mediterranean, to the Ariège, which mingles with the Garonne and flows into the Bay of Biscay. Francis I planned, had death not cheated him of the honor, to assist his subjects by accomplishing this feat which would have added no less to his reputation than had his victories on the battlefield.

It would also be easy to shorten the route from the Caspian Sea to the Mediterranean Sea by cutting out a small piece of land from the Don through the Sea of Azov and the Black Sea to the Volga which flows into the Caspian Sea, for in many places these two rivers flow very close to each other. This would make commerce with Muscovy and the Indies much easier and freer.

I admit that such projects are ambitious and difficult, but they are worthy of great monarchs who should devote themselves in time of peace only to deeds that win public acclaim, to actions that are outstanding, noble, and profitable for the general public. This is such

a project, for it contributes to the establishment and ease of trade. Would it not be pleasant to see men
traveling freely from place to place, communicating 36
with one another with no thought to country, ceremonies, or other such matters, as if men finally realized that the earth is a city common to all? Only savages or thieves would impede so great a good, and it is quite possible that if they were to see themselves alone, even they would think of their own consciences. If they should prefer to continue to live in their own savage fashion, they would not be sufficiently strong to resist so many people who are bound closely by common consent. These good people would descend upon them, hem them in, attack, and kill them like miserable beasts in their lairs. War will always be a just measure against them if they cannot be brought to reason.

Robbers are easily conquered on land either with force or with famine by cutting off their supplies if by chance they should hold inaccessible positions, as is so frequently the case. Pirates are more difficult to capture because of the great expanse of the sea where they find
asylum and refuge. To accomplish this conquest there 37
are two quite dissimilar means: liberality and force. Pompey used both against the Corsairs who were in control of the Mediterranean Sea, and who had reduced Italy to extreme want. After having equipped a goodly number of ships, he set out after them, defeated some and forced the others to accept the conditions he proposed. Then, taking away the ports in which they had been based, he scattered them by leasing them lands in different countries as a means of support. Thus he

broke up their union, which while it lasted, had made them invincible.

If the kings and potentates of today could come to an understanding among themselves, they could, in very little time, rid the seas of these brigands. It is scandalous that we not only tolerate them but even give them rather valuable strongholds, like Algiers and Barbary, as places of refuge. The Sultan reaps little profit and less honor from these dealings. Even though such people can
38 be useful to him on occasion, it would still be more proper for him to place a garrison of brave and honorable soldiers in his cities than to declare himself so openly the protector of the Corsairs. Moreover, peace would relieve him of the necessity of placing himself in such a position, and other monarchs would, for their part, use all of their power to exterminate the thieves.

I would, nevertheless, be tempted to try peaceful means first and to offer them an honest wage. Poverty forces many to lead a dishonest life; if this cause were removed, they would submit to the same policy that governs the general public. The important thing is to provide them with an allowance or rather give them estates. There are so many lands that are useless because they are not cultivated. If they were reclaimed they would serve to feed many of the poor. There are likewise many marshlands that would make fertile fields if they were drained. This idea led the Romans to commission several Magistrates to clear and dry that great alluvian plane on the road to Naples. But they
39 went about it too slowly with the result that the region, which could be converted into fertile prairies or acreage for wheat if only men wanted to work on it, is still full

of mud today. I would say the same about the swamps and desert lands of Languedoc, Provence, and other areas of the realm. This is something that is indicative either of poor management or negligence on the part of the French. There is no difficulty here that cannot be overcome by hard work and perseverance. Nothing is impossible if men are willing to work at it. The Egyptians put this much time and money into their pyramids which were only for show. Is there not all the more reason to make an effort to create fertile fields out of unproductive ones for the benefit of great numbers of poor people?

In case these lands are neither suitable nor sufficient for the pirates, then arable lands must be purchased and given to them on condition that they maintain them properly and pay a small rent to show their gratitude.
This gift would be bought at public expense, but the 40
public would also profit from it. Peace is sometimes purchased from the enemy at a very high price. Why not ward off the evil designs of those who have declared war on the whole world? Why not soften their hearts and make them less aggressive? Why not persuade them through your honest generosity to lead a peaceful life?

There are some people who cannot be won over in any other way, like those two rocks of which Pliny spoke, that will not budge when they are shoved but sway when touched lightly with a finger. Some men can be brought to reason by peaceful means who cannot be swayed by any amount of violence. There is no greater or more secure victory than that won by courtesy and mercy. A ruler will never be blamed for seeking, by whatever means, his own and his subjects' profit. The

Emperor Soliman made a masterful diplomatic stroke when he reached an agreement with the arch-pirates Dragut and Barbarossa. He welcomed them in his Council, gave them governments and honorable positions in order to have peace in his empire. In short,
41 he made good friends out of powerful enemies. This method of winning the Corsairs to virtue is deserving of praise. Its end result is two-fold: that by their example others may be brought to a sense of their own duty and that despair may not incite them to commit even greater cruelties.

If, however, some wish to continue their thievery, they must be pursued and punished without mercy. Every ruler should keep a few ships ready for the purpose of fighting off these sea monsters. Augustus saw to this matter very well. Besides the ships that he had in the ports of Ostia, Fréjus, and on the Rhine, Danube, and Euphrates, he maintained two large fleets, one at Messina which guarded the coasts of France, Spain, Africa, Egypt, Sardinia, and Sicily, the other at Ravenna that cruised in the waters of Greece and the Orient.

The safety of sea routes depends entirely on the present monarchs. It will bring them both honor and personal gain. The King of Spain is conscientious about this, for his lieutenant at Goa sails the East Indian
42 Ocean every year with an army of men in order to prevent pirate raids. And to this same end, he maintains a good garrison in the city of Santo Domingo which, because of its geographical location, commands the Caribbean Sea. Other kings could do the same thing to free their shores from piracies, and when commerce has thus been established, men will have an excellent

opportunity to take up trade either on land or at sea.

If anyone feels that he is not suited or predisposed to business, there are other trades appropriate for the ordinary person. These other trades should not be scorned, for architecture, painting, the goldsmith's trade, clock making, or the making of silks and linens, and other arts referred to as mechanical, require almost as much originality and skill as the liberal arts and are far more practical. For this reason it would be a good idea to encourage artisans, to offer them rewards for their work, and to establish an officer in every city who would record the names of those who excelled in some 43
art. In this way, one could give them work commensurate with their abilities which would have to be demonstrated in the presence of a master craftsman. This policy would stimulate people, make them less lethargic, and make them glad to take up a vocation in the hope that they would be well provided for on condition that they acquit themselves well.

The greatest encouragement of all would be the interest shown by the Magistrate in their profession, for there is nothing that encourages virtue or industry more than rewards given by a public figure. Then there would be healthy competition among men of the same trade. Each would strive to surpass his neighbor in order to win the reputation and certificates earned by anyone who has done well in his trade.

But this state of affairs is not imminent. The arts are scorned both individually and collectively. There is almost no way at present to earn a comfortable living by honest means. A man, no matter how great the industry, knowledge, or skill he may have in his trade, is no more

44 respected than a mere apprentice. Nor does he know to whom to turn in order to find some way of earning his living if he has no other patron or security than his own competence. To whom shall he turn? To his peers? Jealousy would prevent them from wishing him well. Even though he may create miracles, he is not allowed to have a shop of his own if he does not have the money to be admitted as a master. This custom could no doubt supress all the arts, and might make idlers out of men who would prefer to walk the streets, hire themselves out as strong-arm men and cutthroats, or beg rather than work since good and creative workers are not rewarded.

The mechanical arts must therefore be encouraged, and the above-mentioned regulations should be applied to them so that the common people will enter them in the hope of making a profit and attaining a suitable standard of living. Lycurgus was wrong in forbidding his people to take up manual labor and trade, for all they had left was the sword and buckler. To do this was to violate human society, to take away every form of
45 beauty, and even to deprive it of the ordinary necessities. His ruling was good only for a republic of beasts who have only tooth and claw. Numa behaved more wisely when he divided the people of Rome into brotherhoods and established one for each trade. He recognized that the foundation of a city is composed of artisans and merchants and that without them a state cannot survive, but will disintegrate.

I shall leave to your imagination the difficulties in which we would find ourselves if we had no laborers, vinyardmen, weavers, tanners, iron workers, smiths,

surgeons, dyers, masons, carpenters, founders, shoemakers, fullers, rope makers, silversmiths, potters, turners, and other such workers on whom not only our luxuries, but our very lives depend. To say that such occupations are suitable only for slaves, as Lycurgus thought, is impertinent, for a prudent and gracious man never scorns anything he cannot do without. Why should the mechanical arts be scorned, especially those that give evidence of some skill apart from the profit
and pleasure they bring? Besides, it is not the position 46
that brings honor to the man, but the man who brings honor to the position, as Epaminondus said when he was given a lowly commission quite unsuited to his abilities.

Nonetheless, men qualified either by social rank or by keenness of mind should devote themselves to the sciences, above all to those sciences which have some usefulness in life, namely Medicine and Mathematics. As for the latter, it cannot be recommended too highly if we consider the scope of its purpose and the grandeur of its accomplishments besides the certainty of its proofs and the ease which long ago encouraged children to study it. As for medicine, although many belittle it, its utility is obvious. For every reason put forth to downgrade it, there are a hundred that could be used to defend it. Let us look at some other branches of knowledge. Theology surpasses our ability. Dialectics is only servant and gate-keeper to the others. Physics is a
knowledge of nature and depends on experimentation. 47
Rhetoric is superfluous. Jurisprudence is equally unnecessary, and good common sense suffices to clear up lawsuits without having recourse to a multiplicity of laws and decisions that serve only to confuse rather than

to clarify issues. Grammar, poetry, and history are more lofty than practical. So much so that among all the honest disciplines, grammar and poetry hold first place in the mind of the general public. And yet these ought to be recommended without prejudicing other disciplines which also form a part of the background of a liberally educated man. This is the sort of activity in which rulers could require their subjects to participate, so that they would have something with which to occupy themselves, and thus would not spend their time disturbing the peace.

And so we have rejected all the causes and pretexts of war. Still one other consideration remains before us: the matter of the enmity, and if we must say so, the antipathy among some peoples which originated either in old quarrels or in differences of opinion with respect
48 to religious beliefs. How is it possible, someone will ask, to establish harmony among peoples who are so far removed both in their goals and in their loyalties. For example: the Turk and the Persian, the Frenchman and the Spaniard, the Chinaman and the Tartar, the Christian and the Jew, or the Mohammedan? I contend that such hostilities are only political and cannot erase the bond that exists and ought to continue to exist among men. The distances that separate domiciles cannot lessen in any way the ties created by blood, nor can they take away the basic similarity in men's nature which is the true foundation of friendship and human society. Why should I, a Frenchman, wish to harm an Englishman, a Spaniard, or an Indian? I cannot when I consider that they are men as I am, and that just as they, I am subject to error and sin, and that all nations

are joined by a natural and therefore insoluble bond.
This tie means that one man cannot call another an
alien unless he follows the common, deeply-rooted
prejudice passed down from generation to generation.

The same applies to religions which do so much to
arouse men and set them against one another. 49
Consequently, the Christian, when he meets a Jew or a
Mohammedan, thinks he has been contaminated by
their very presence and that he has seen a demon. On
the other hand, both these people and the pagans
despise the Christian just as much. I have mentioned
these four religions because they are the most common,
and all the others hinge on them. Christians accuse the
Mohammedans of superstitions and ridiculous beliefs.
These in turn accuse the Christians of blasphemy and
impiety and never speak of them except with scorn. The
pagans boast of the antiquity of their rites and consider
themselves fortunate to be able to continue with their
sacrifices. The Jews ridicule all that. And yet, although
they are hated and expelled from one country after
another, they draw the conclusion that all this is a mark
of blessing and divine favor because, in the midst of so
many enemies and persecutions, they have survived and
continue to do so despite the many attacks and assaults
they have had to withstand. Historians praise the
Messenians because, although they spent 300 years as 50
refugees in a foreign land, they did not change their
language or ancient customs in any way. The case of the
Jews is even more amazing, since they have steadfastly
persevered in the faith of their fathers for centuries.

Now all these religions are based on proofs; all cite
their own miracles, and every man presumes his religion

to be the best. I have not undertaken to settle these differences. A better man than I would be at a loss to do so. I should like to say only that they all strive for the same end, namely the recognition and adoration of a divinity. If some do not choose the right road or the right means, it is through ignorance and poor teaching rather than malice. Consequently, they should be treated with compassion rather than hatred. Is it really necessary to wage war because of differences in ceremony? I shall not say in religion, since its principal goal lies in the adoration of God.

In the matter of religion, the heart plays a greater role than do the exterior forms and sacrifices of which men
51 make so great a display. I do not pretend to conclude that one should scorn ritual; but I do contend that we should not persecute those who do not wish to conform to our ways. The law of Moses forbids slandering foreign gods, and in the temple of Solomon they did not have any qualms about receiving the offerings of idolaters. Now men delight in destroying those who do not agree with their faith. They try them and with words condemn them, not to ordinary punishments, but to everlasting damnation.

Piety is too good a tree to bear such evil fruit as malice, hostility, and slander. This virtue, like all others, must be accompanied by prudence for fear that the same thing should happen to us as happened to Apuleius, who, trying to change into a bird, found that he had been transformed into an ass. Therefore, while we are trying to gain heaven through religion, let us be careful not to fall instead into stupidity and brutal inhumanity. I am accusing no one in particular, nor do I

specify *any one religion*, but the fact remains that there are many who can be compared to Ulysses' companions who thought they had discovered a rich treasure, only to discover that it was nothing but a bag of wind. 52
Conceit blinds everyone and transforms him into a second Narcissus with the result that he is lost in self love. The truth of the pastoral song, "Often the ugly thing is beautiful to an admirer," is confirmed again and again.

If we were even content to favor our own customs, there would be no cause for astonishment or complaint, but in this we are unlike other lovers who do not desire rivals. On the contrary, we want everyone to embrace our own beliefs as an infallible rule. This vice is common to ordinary people who have never traveled farther than the outskirts of their own city. They think that everyone must needs live as they and value no other customs but theirs. Thus they resemble those simpletons of Athens who thought that the moon shining in their country was more beautiful than the one shining in others. As a Persian gentleman said to Themistocles, wise and holy men look beyond and consider that the harmony of the world is composed of differing opinions and that what is praiseworthy in one place is not thought to be good everywhere.

This reminds me of what Aelian relates about two 53
cities in the new world whose policies are very different. In the first, the inhabitants practice justice and have uninterrupted peace; for this reason it is called Pious. The other is named Valiant; its inhabitants are always armed and are continuously waging war since they are incapable of living in peace. This is shown by the fact

that they once crossed the ocean to conquer our lands. When they were advised that the people in this part of the world, that is, in Asia, Europe, and Africa believed strongly in religion, they decided against carrying out their plan. It is as if they would have been ashamed to discover such credulity in an unknown people.

Everyone may draw his own conclusions from this story. The important thing is that people recognize that men are very different, and that what one group of people esteems, another may despise or ridicule. In my opinion, this is what caused some philosophers to hold that honesty and turpitude are only fantasy and a matter of common agreement among men. They were
54 dreamers. I believe this to be so, especially as far as this proposition is concerned.

But it is not enough to note the vices of this or that person. We must also consider our own, and not do as that fairy did who put on her eyes as she entered her neighbors' houses, but upon arriving home hung them up at the door. If curiosity makes us prone to criticize someone else's behavior, at least let us, after enumerating his defects, look also at his good qualities. Let us not do as the Ophiogenes did and suck the venom from deeds. Let us not be like flies either which tend to stop on rough and contaminated surfaces rather than on clean and polished ones.

I believe that those people who do not follow the true religion are impious, that their belief is absurd and blasphemous. Nevertheless, they are men as we, cast in the same mould and created by the same Workman, capable of reason and of the moral virtues which may make them deserving of friendship and admiration if

only we do not allow ourselves to become blinded by
prejudice and overconfidence. Let us reject these two 55
step-children of the mind, these twins born of our stupidity which seal the eyes of human understanding and impede those good inclinations given us by nature. Let us keep clearly in mind that religion is not made up of words and appearances. It is not enough to say "I have true faith, I attend sacrifices and public prayers." One must be a good man and have charity, without which faith is useless. Anyone lacking this virtue does not have religion engraven in his heart.

Some serve God out of hypocrisy. Many believe in Him through hearsay or habit; but when one sees devotion coupled with gentleness and charity, that is the sign of a truly religious soul. Piety is incompatible with animosity. If we are on the road to salvation, good. Let us try by instruction and good example to bring others to it. There are no other means to uproot the errors and
false opinions that men have conjured up in their minds 56
with respect to things devine. Slander and malicious criticism have no effect on them; force is useless. Are we not aware of this? It would indeed be better if there were only one form of worship, the diversity of rituals and rites divides the loyalties of peoples and often leads them to form factions. In fact, wise rulers oppose new religions that are trying to gain a footing, but they tolerate those that have already acquired a considerable following and are firmly rooted. In the first instance, zeal motivates them; in the second, necessity obliges them. They also see the truth of the maxim that war, being the source of all villanies, impieties, blasphemies, and atheism, weakens true religion instead of advancing

it and can also bring about the ruin of the state.

I shall not hold, as Symmachus did, that the way one discovers divine truth is of no importance. Still less would I want to maintain that all religions are founded by human means, as a contemporary theologian who is otherwise a great defender of the Roman Catholic Church has done. The result of such a contention would
57 be to judge them all by the same standard and to call the three truths into question, since every man is liable to deceive and to be mistaken. Certainly there is one confession of faith and one form of ritual more acceptable than the others. Since, however, this is a supernatural grace, it must come from God and not from men who, with all their might, do not have the power to make anyone believe the smallest article of their mysteries. They may make a few go to the temple, the synagogue, or the mosque, but such violence will create hypocrites, not believers. Let them who have the true religion, therefore, thank God for this grace and strive to show it by good works. Let them not try arrogantly to bend to their will others in whose beliefs they are not at all interested, provided of course that these other persons keep themselves within the bounds of modesty and do not disturb the peace.

This is the goal toward which we must strive. Men are
58 not responsible for punishing or correcting defects in faith. It is up to Him who sees men's hearts and their most secret thoughts. Willful wrongs are punishable under civil laws. Those related to understanding, that is, false doctrine, have God alone as judge. Therefore, those who have tried to strike this cord have gained nothing by it. The Emperor Charles V, a zealous supporter of his

religion if there ever was one, tried to smother Lutheranism in its very beginnings. To this end he used the forces of Spain, Italy, Germany, and the Netherlands. He won battles from the Protestants, took their leaders prisoner, and gave this new sect such a setback that it was on the point of being checked. All at once, fortune changed. This Antaeus whom he had thrown to the ground arose from his fall with redoubled strength. Now he has a new enemy on his hands. His allies rebel. He is more hindered after his victory than before; in a word, he is forced, in order to preserve his own state, to give the vanquished what they asked: freedom of conscience.

The same thing has happened to our kings who have
tried by every possible means to rally their subjects to 59
the old faith. They have pursued its enemies with fire and sword, have overwhelmed them in many encounters. Then they recognized the fact that it was easier to maintain two religions in peace than to preserve one by war and that such a difference in faith was not prejudicial to peaceful co-existence. Thus we see that the Turks live in peace even though they permit the practice of other religions besides Mohammedanism. The Poles are not upset by this diversity. The King of Spain allows freedom of conscience in the Indies. All this goes to show that differences in religion are not serious impediments to universal peace. But it is not enough to establish it. We need to guarantee it in perpetuity, which is very difficult.

To come to an agreement, one needs only a good idea that will touch the hearts of rulers, or else the persuasive power of a man of authority to reconcile them.

Sometimes, in fact, necessity will oblige them to come to an agreement after they have harassed one another. It seems, though, that a calm can never last long on the
60 ocean of our relations where the impetuous winds of ambition arouse so many storms. Let us suppose for a moment that the peace treaty is signed today; that it is published in the open arena of the world. How do we know whether posterity will ratify the articles it contains? Desires are changeable, and the actions of men today are in no way binding upon their successors. To cut short this objection, we need only remember what we have said concerning the causes of war. Since they are not insurmountable, for the reasons stated above, there is nothing that could bring about a disruption of the peace.

Nevertheless, in order to avoid petty disturbances, a city should be chosen where all sovereigns would always have ambassadors so that any differences that should arise would be settled by a decision of the whole assembly. The ambassadors of the parties involved would set forth their masters' complaints, and the other deputies would judge them dispassionately. To give more weight to this decision, advice would be sought
61 from the great republics too, for these nations would also have their ministers in the same place. I mean the great republics, like those of the Venetians and the Swiss, not those petty states that are unable to stand alone and must depend on others for protection. If anyone should refuse to follow the decision of such an august body, he would incur the ill-will of all the other rulers who would certainly have the means to bring him back to the path of reason.

Now the most suitable place for such an assembly would be the territory of Venice, since it is neutral and not partial to any ruler. Another advantage is its location. It is situated near the most powerful monarchies on earth: the Pope, the two emperors, and the King of Spain. It is not far from France, Tartary, Muscovy, Poland, England, and Denmark. As for Persia, China, Ethiopia, and the East and West Indies, they are indeed far removed from the others, but navigation can overcome this difficulty, and no one should refuse to make the long trip for such a worthy purpose. Therefore, I can see no other place in the world more suitable for such a meeting than this city.

The more difficult task will be in determining the 62
rank to be given to such ambassadors, for they will not yield easily to one another. Nevertheless, I shall give my opinion on the matter, not that I consider myself capable of such arbitration, but because it is important to clarify this point with respect to our discussion. Everyone else is welcome to give his opinion on it too. If I followed my own inclinations, and my desires should be realized, then, because of the respect that every good man owes his religion and his country, as a Roman Catholic and a Frenchman, I know what I should say. But one cannot think only of oneself when it is a matter of securing the well-being of the whole society of mankind to which we all belong, of permitting no one to be dissatisfied, or of giving every man his rightful place. I shall speak objectively, then, as if I had been born in Plato's imaginary Republic or in the realm of his Ideas. If any monarch should conclude that I have given too much importance to others and in

63 so doing have jeopardized his position, I should beg His Majesty to believe that I did it unaware of his true greatness. In this matter I am following only the most common and frequently expressed opinions.

I am sure that few people would deny the first place to the Pope: First, because of the honor that all Christian rulers pay him, second because of the deference that almost all of them accord him in spiritual matters and third because of the respect due ancient Rome of which he is the temporal lord. For these reasons, the first place in all assemblies belongs to him or to his deputy.

As for the second place, if we accept the principle that honor should be attributed to princes in proportion to the majesty, power, and prosperity of their monarchies, such qualities are so pre-eminent in the Turkish Emperor that no one can deny him the second position. There is also the fact that he holds the city of Constantinople, the seat of the eastern empire, which is the counterpart of Rome: therefore it bears the same name. These considerations will induce the Christian Emperor, who would perhaps like to contest this right, to accept the third place as willingly as the other
64 monarchs will freely allow him to occupy it. For although kings receive their scepters from God alone, while their name is august, their person sacred and inviolable, nevertheless, the title "Emperor" has always been deemed more exalted and formidable.

Thus it seems that those men were mistaken who wrote that the Emperor is no more than a simple leader having no greater authority than a duke of Venice and that the sovereignty of the empire which formerly

resided in the senate and the people now rests with the German States. To support their statement, they cite the example of two or three emperors who were deposed. This argument, however, is not valid since we can read of many kings who have similarly been deprived of their scepters, and whose successors have nevertheless been recognized as sovereigns. If a few emperors have subordinated the authority vested in them to the assembly of the states, if they now act only on the advice of the assembly's counsel, we must not conclude from this that they have thereby lost their sovereignty anymore than kings who allow their edicts to be examined and ratified by a Council or Parliament. 65
Submission accepted voluntarily must not be taken as a precedent. For every prince who has allowed himself to be subjected either because of modesty or lack of concern, one can cite a dozen who have acted differently and have not allowed their power to be diminished in any way. The election of the emperor and the respect he pays the pope are formalities that do not detract from his greatness in the least.

Moreover, in order to judge something, one must do it primarily on the basis of its origins and initial establishment and not on any changes it has subsequently undergone. Now if we consider the emperors of ancient times, we shall have no doubt at all that they were sovereigns. Julius Caesar, who was the first to take this title, said that the Republic was no longer anything but a meaningless name, and that everyone must now consider his word inviolate. Augustus was no less a sovereign, and even the people yielded their power to him. I would say the same for

other emperors. If they sought the advice of the senate or if they justified their actions, it was not because they were obliged to do so but because of real or false
66 modesty. What greater sign of sovereignty could be desired than the absolute power to command, to order everything to suit him, even the lives of his subjects, to bestow kingdoms and to be answerable to no one?

Emperors have enjoyed all of these rights. If they have allowed their authority to be dissipated, it does not follow that the title they bear, given its true meaning, signifies only Captain-in-Chief, as Bodin would have us think. I am very well aware that it was true at the time when the Romans were free. At that time a general was given the title "emperor," especially after having won some outstanding victory, and he bore this title only for a short time as his surname. But Julius Caesar, having supplanted all his enemies and seized control of Rome, gave new importance to this title, and took it as a first name so that he might be considered noble. As historians have brought out, this act earned him the envy and hatred of many.

To speak of our own times, kings would not be respected for conceding, as they do, to this Prince if
67 they considered him merely a lieutenant or someone else's subject. The French kings, who formerly held the Empire, and who indeed gained it by the strength of their arms, are deeply involved in this question. Thus their claim to precedence, at least over other kings, cannot be debated, for they govern one of the most renowned nations in the world today. Whether we speak of the ancient Gauls whose conquests are well-known and whose tribes, established throughout the land, give

sufficient testimony to their valor, or whether we consider the Frenchmen who are their descendants, their name is still today one to be reckoned with. It is better known to foreign countries than any other name. Thus these nations will willingly concede the fourth place to the monarch of so great a kingdom.

After him, I shall not hesitate to place the king of Spain whose power and riches equal those of the greatest of kings and whose kingdom is larger than theirs. For the sixth place there might arise a debate among the kings of Persia and China, Prester John, the Precop of Tartary, and the Grand Duke of Muscovy.
Nonetheless, when I consider that the Persians at one 68
time were *the* monarchy in all the world, and that they still hold a good share of their former domain, I feel that they ought to take precedence over the Ethiopians who in turn should precede the Tartars. The Tartan empire dates back only three or four centuries, and Prester John's empire can boast of its antiquity besides other things it has to recommend it. Because of his opulence and even more because of the exemplary administration of his kingdom, the king of China, after the Tartars, deserves a place in the consistory of sovereigns. The Duke or Emperor of Muscovy equals or surpasses him in military strength. The kings of Great Britain, Poland, Denmark, Sweden, Japan, Morocco, the Great Mogul, and other monarchs from the Indies or Africa should not hold the least important places. All noble princes, who are self-sufficient, and do not
depend on anyone else, could contest the honor 69
bestowed on them by their rank in the consistory with their peers.

Still, since in all assemblies some order must be maintained, I cannot conceive of any plan better or more reasonable than the one I have proposed. If some princes are not happy with it, then let them appeal to the judgment of the others. This procedure would in no way diminish their authority. On the contrary, they will be all the more esteemed if they voluntarily submit to reason. For it must not be admitted that reason is on the point of a sword. That kind of empty bluster is fit only for savages. The ancient Gauls found that they had done the wrong thing when they told the Roman ambassadors that everything belonged to the strongest. The fatal result of their stand shows very clearly that those who refuse to recognize reason as their mistress fall, in the end, into the hands of their enemies. The adversaries conquer them by quite different means and show them what happens when they rely on mere bravado.

It appears that no sovereign, whoever he may be, should hesitate to bow to the judgment of so many sovereigns not only concerning this matter but also
70 concerning any other difference he might need to work out with his peers. If the opinions of the assembly of princes or their deputies should be found to be equally divided on some question, as can happen, then the deputies of the Republics, who would have the right to speak and to vote, could be polled in order to terminate the debate by giving their support to one side or the other.

Inasmuch as there are a number of princes whose majesty, power, and wealth are equal, and consequently none of whom will want to yield precedence to the

other, I think that it would be well to order, as is done in some places, that the first among them to arrive or else the oldest should have precedence. A better alternative is to imitate the Roman Consuls who each took command in turn. In this way they would share the disputed place and each would fill it successively. This would be one way of obviating any discontent, but this procedure would be necessary only for those who are vying for the same place. It is not reasonable that
the king of a city or a little province should try to reach 71
a compromise with a French or Spanish king. Still less should a duke, marquis, or count attempt it. I am confident that the Dukes of Florence, Lorraine, and Savoy, although they are sovereigns, will nevertheless consider themselves honored to have a seat in such an assembly after those who bear the title "king," particularly after those kings who have not usurped this title recently through their ambitious manoeuvres. Therefore, if differences of opinion over the question of precedence should arise, they will occur between persons of similar rank, that is, Dukes, Marquises, and Counts. I do not intend to make any distinction among these ranks, because I believe that while Duke is ordinarily the highest of the three, nevertheless, it often happens that a Count or Marquis has Dukes who hold lands from him. And too, there are many considerations more important than a mere title, for instance, the reputation, antiquity, power, and extent of a given monarchy. These are the essential points to consider when according honor and precedence. Following these
general guidelines, the kings and emperors will judge any 72
disputes among the said lesser princes and will assign to

each his proper place which, it is assumed, he will accept graciously.

What prince would be so foolhardy as to dare to go counter to the company of the world's monarchs? The cities of Greece all yielded to the decree of the Amphictyonic League, and those who did not obey them incurred general censure, not only from their countrymen, but also from foreigners. This was proven by the fact that Philip of Macedon found a pretext to wage a cruel war against the inhabitants of Phocis because they had been condemned by the League. The ancient princes of Gaul, although they kept their domains and sovereignty separate, submitted their differences to the Druids on pain of being excommunicated and hated by all the people. And yet there has never been a more august or more honorable body than the one of which we are speaking, a body composed of the ambassadors of all monarchies and
73 sovereign republics who would be the trustees and guarantees for world peace.

To give this assembly more authority, all the said princes would swear to consider as inviolable any law passed by the majority of votes cast and to take up arms against those who sought to oppose it. The council, then, would judge debates not only on precedence, but also on other matters that might arise and would try to keep everyone on good terms with one another. It would attempt to anticipate causes of discontent and smooth them over by peaceful means if possible, by force if necessary.

Having established peace generally among all princes in this way, the only remaining problem would be to

maintain it specifically in each particular monarchy. Individual monarchs would all work to this end and should not have too much difficulty either in holding their own people in check or in exacting obedience from them. What ordinarily forces monarchs to concede to their subjects is either the fear that the people may ally themselves with foreign powers or that the latter may take advantage of internal factions or quarrels. Now if
world peace were established, this fear would cease to 74
exist. Everyone would content himself with his own domain and would concentrate on governing his own people. A prince would be adulated by good men, and the wicked would tremble at his sight. He would not need to fear rebellions and factions to which he could quickly put a stop with the assistance of the other sovereigns who, all having a vested interest in the punishment of rebels, would promptly send him help.

Thus the princes would reap the primary benefit of universal peace. They can certainly do nothing in the present situation. Let them fortify themselves through alliances as much as they like, build strongholds and arm themselves on every side. They will always have cause for fear if they do not come to a common agreement for world peace. One enemy prince is all that is needed to dispossess them. Not only a neighbor, but also a distant people, often one no one suspected, is capable of ruining a monarchy. The name "Macedonian" was
obscure and unknown until the time of Philip and 75
Alexander who subdued all of the Orient. The Goths stayed virtually in hiding in a remote corner of Germany until the reign of Valentinian, at which time they began to spread out over the country so successfully that in a

few years they made a clean sweep of the Roman Empire. The Angles were held in no higher esteem than the pirates of the same time, but this did not prevent their seizing Great Britain. People began hearing of the French less than fourteen hundred years ago. The Turks rose up during the time of the Emperor Basil, and they became even more active under Constantine the Gladiator. The Tartars have made their presence felt for three or four hundred years now. If at the time that these people left their country there had been world peace, others would certainly have prevented their expanding as far as they did. Armies would have arrived from every country to attack them, and they would not have been able to resist the whole universe allied against them. But they saw their opportunity, given the divisions existing among other peoples who were happy to see their neighbors destroyed and abandoned them, when necessary, since there were no alliances or treaties of mutual friendship.

76 Let us always be afraid that what we have done to others will happen to us. We do not yet know all the countries in the inhabitable parts of the world. There is perhaps a people somewhere in the west or the south who is cutting out our work for us. If anyone had told the Americans 150 years ago that bearded men would soon come to conquer their country, they would have paid no attention to this warning other than to make a joke of it. They saw in a moment what they had not foreseen, and, before hearing the name of the Spaniards, they felt their power in exactly the same way as a flash of lightning appears before a clap of thunder. The distance between places, the difficulty of the route, the

width of that terrible ocean which had been a natural rampart for them, none of these were proof against a destruction that would be incredible if its effects were not clearly visible.

What a strange thing! Imagine seeing three hundred men enter an unknown land abounding in riches and people, build forts there without opposition, then impose their law on so many millions of men, take and
kill their kings, and finally reduce a rich world to 77
wretched servitude. It passes all belief. Shall we say that they were cowards who had neither courage nor valor? All very well, but history does not speak of them that way. On the contrary it attests to the fact that most of these people were much given to warlike pursuits. Even if they had been weak from every point of view, it is certain that Cortez, with only 900 Spaniards, would have been incapable of conquering all the Mexicans if he had not been favored by their enemies who aided his cause by giving him 200,000 men.

Thus the factions within the country opened the door to foreigners who took over all of them. If the various states of this new world had been at peace with one another, if their leaders had been satisfied with their own domains, they would still be living in freedom. But they could not be happy unless they were despoiling their neighbors; they wanted the honor of bringing them under their command and of extending their monarchy
as far as their javelins could reach. This ambition was 78
their ruin. All this should demonstrate clearly enough that nothing can make an empire secure except a general peace of which the chief ingredient is the territorial limitation of monarchies.

Thus each prince must remain within the boundaries of the lands he now possesses, and he must not go beyond them on any pretext. If any feels cheated by such a regulation, let him consider that the boundaries of kingdoms and principalities are set by the hand of God, Who takes them away and transfers them as He sees fit. Let him remember that if his father or grandfather was powerful, his great-grandfather and other ancestors were private citizens. Therefore, let no prince dream of recovering what God lent his family for a time, but rather let him conserve what he still has and not risk the certain for the uncertain.

In short, to return to our proposition, if he has some cause for complaint, let him present his arguments to
79 the general assembly as the most competent judge imaginable. This is the principal means of establishing world peace, and the one on which all the others depend. This is where we must begin. For as long as sovereigns keep to themselves and have no communication with each other through their ambassadors, they will try to expand their kingdoms whatever the price, and will always find a sufficient pretext for encroaching upon one another. If, however, they are satisfied with their present fortune, if they pay the just claims of their people as they ought to do, if they unite within the framework of this assembly of which they will constitute the membership, there will be nothing that can delay or disrupt a just peace. There is no point in saying that the wicked will prevent this from happening and that they always exist in larger numbers than the good. This argument is false; but if it were true, all would be lost. To what lengths will wickedness not

go when it is backed by power?

When I consider the state of human affairs, I find that
mankind is divided into three approximately equal 80
parts. This division can be found in every province, city,
and village. Some men are evil; some are good; and the
rest are weaklings. Under the heading of weaklings I
include those who are weak either in mind or in body
and especially timid men whom I have separated from
the good, because timidity prevents an infinite number
of virtuous acts. That is why an old proverb advises us
not to burden ourselves with the faint-hearted. Actually,
such people do neither good nor evil, but always side
with the strongest. As for the wicked, they do not dare
show their ill-will unless they have a leader who
sanctions it. That is when they launch their campaign.
Otherwise their efforts, like a thief's, are short-lived.

How then can they prevent peace when they see all
the princes aided by all the men of good will who will
be certain to come to the prince's aid in this worthy
cause? As for the weaklings, are they not just as desirous
of peace? The two thirds will no doubt win out over the 81
other, and you will see all these firebrands bend like a
glove to the wishes of their monarchs. Just let the
proclamation of peace read *by order of the king*, and
these words will make the weapons drop from their
hands.

There might be some difficulty in bringing the Turks and the Tartars to adopt a peaceable life, for they do not willingly indulge in any exercise but war. But these people are so subservient to the authority of their princes that, seeing them resolved to make peace, they will not dare to contradict them. Since they have such

outstanding empires, these two monarchs need not wage
war. And what will they do if they see that all the other
princes are in agreement? No! No! We are no longer
living in an age when one should be dreaming of
trophies to be won. We must do away with these
barbarous customs and show the people the road to
humanity and true honor so that they will not continue
to live so brutally. We must establish the reign of reason
and justice, and not violence, which is fit only for
beasts. In the past men have been most free with human
82 life. We have seen a universal deluge of their blood
capable of turning the land and sea red. Enough. It was
a bloodletting necessary to purge the world of its vicious
and superfluous humors, and God wanted to use this
means to establish monarchies. Now that they are firmly
resting on the pilings of long possession, they must not
be shaken, but rather reinforced by lasting peace.
Soliman the Magnificent gave away kingdoms with a
liberal hand, saying that he was satiated with all the
glory that his virtue and that of his ancestors had
acquired. Perhaps he learned that from Caesar who
became almost indifferent to new conquests and no
longer yearned for them. Whatever the reason, doing evil
becomes tiresome. Let us put the sword back in its
scabbard. Let us no longer try to immortalize our
animosities. We have stirred up enough storms. Now is
the time to try to bring calm and serenity to this great
ocean by throwing on it the oil of complete
reconciliation.

This depends on your Majesties, Great Monarchs. You
now have the opportunity to alleviate all the troubles in
83 the world and to make your peoples obey the laws of

nature and your own. What more could you ask? Peace will guarantee you your present greatness, respect, and security while war weakens all of these and often takes them away altogether along with life and honor. If you were to conquer the whole world, which never has been and never will be done, you would finally be forced to rest, since war is waged to obtain peace. What you would do in your universal monarchy, do now with your present monarchy. You see how little profit there is in the use of arms, and if you conquer some city, you lose it or one more valuable in very little time. Often, after having defeated your enemies and ravaged their lands, necessity forces you to agree to a peace or truce for lack of supplies. Or else a disease decimates an army, and you end up losing the benefits of a hard-won conquest which is ordinarily more expensive than if you had just bought the land outright.

This reminds me of the time the King of Portugal was 84
debating whether or not to send an expedition into Africa. Someone told him that it would take a world of men, money and supplies. This set forth very well, in a few words, the difficulties and perils of war. Octavius Augustus, the greatest monarch who ever lived, never advised undertaking a war unless there was more profit to be gained from victory than possible loss to be incurred from defeat. He contended that to do otherwise was to fish with a golden hook. This is why the Scythians informed Cyrus, King of Persia, that they were amazed that so rich a prince would attack them so blithely without ever having been offended by them, for in so doing he put his own state in jeopardy when all that there was to gain was a poor country. Nevertheless,

they would not stand by and wait for him to come to
them but would gladly go out to meet him on the
battlefield, for they had hopes of gaining such
magnificent spoils. And this they did. The Swiss sent a
85 similar message to the last Duke of Burgundy. If by
chance you conquer us, these poor people said to him,
you will not gain much, considering that the spurs of
your men-at-arms and the bits of their horses' bridles are
worth more than all our wordly goods. This should serve
as a warning to all princes, and especially to powerful
ones, not to try the fortunes of war. They are far more
likely to diminish an empire than to increase it. Let
these monarchs therefore not covet new lands for fear
of losing those they now possess. They have acquired a
certain position. Now they need only manage it well,
following the example of Augustus, who, after calming
troubled areas, set to work to draft good laws. Seeing
that he was secure against foreign invasion, he tried to
forestall any disturbances that might arise within his
own kingdom.

Preventing evil that might come from outside is not
enough. Domestic difficulties can be more perilous. So,
after all the princes have reached an agreement, each
must oversee the affairs of his kingdom so that the
behavior of his own subjects does not endanger the unity
86 we are trying to establish. In so doing, he will not only
benefit his people by contributing toward the
maintenance of a general peace, but his own state will
become secure if he can prevent, through sound policies,
the disturbances that result from a disruption of morals
and unbridled license.

I would be doing the job of a philosopher if I were to

set forth all of the noteworthy teachings on this subject. But there is no need to reconstruct a dialogue which fills books. I shall touch on only seven or eight points that I deem essential for keeping nations in the line of duty and eliminating all pretexts for rebellion. These are: moderate government, the punishment of wickedness, reward for good, provision for the poor, regulation of trials, public provision of grain, lawful recreation, and the power of censure. A state is healthy when all of these conditions are met.

Of these, the first is the most important, as much for
the welfare of the people as for that of the monarch 87
himself. He cannot be secure among his subjects if he does not gain their affection by governing according to the laws of reason, to which every man, without exception, owes obedience. Submission to these laws does not detract in any way from his sovereignty. On the contrary, it frees a man from the vices that would keep him in an unfortunate state of subservience. To reign is to be in control of one's desires.

Every man can easily attain such a *Monarchy*, but princes must be especially careful in this matter, since they have absolute power. Theopompus, a Lacedemonian king, did not need to establish ephors to criticize him. He thought it better to lay down the law for himself rather than to give this function to others who were as fallible as he. Royal authority is not dependent on any superior, thus it requires a noble, virtuous man who models his government on that of the Great Sovereign. It demands one who does not heed flatterers who make princes believe that they need not stop at anything, and who invite them to tyranny as

though being an emperor or a king were synonymous
88 with massacring, pillaging, and blithely doing evil as
thieves do.

A legitimate monarch does not act in this way and considers that the greatest honor that can come to him is to be able to refrain from doing evil. He realizes that just because he has the power, he should not treat his subjects like slaves, or at least he should emulate the Parthians whose slaves were as dear to them as their own children. He will accomplish this by sparing their lives, their honor, and their goods. By knowing his practices in these three areas, one can easily distinguish between a tyrant and a legitimate prince. The latter allows his subjects to enjoy their possessions in peace. If he must take some in the form of taxes, it is always to underwrite projects necessary for the general public and not for his own pleasure. He makes no attempt on their lives, and he does not destroy their honor by taking their women. A tyrannical prince derives pleasure from all of these things and thinks that he can attain happiness through violence. He is mistaken about this. A
violent empire is like torrential rains which quickly run
89 off again, whereas a moderate one is like those gentle
showers which water the land and last a long time.

Thus a good prince, when he has won the hearts of his people, need not be afraid of them. When he perceives that he is justly hated by his own people who are looking for the opportunity to get rid of him, the tyrant is filled with suspicion. This, in part, is what destroyed the kings and potentates of the New World. They persecuted their subjects with intolerable demands for forced labor and governed them like animals. For

this reason the poor wretches made little resistance to
the Spaniards who held out hope for better treatment.
Let a prince handle his subjects as sensibly as he can.
Let him not torment them with bodily afflictions, since
these same bodies are necessary to him. Let him not
demand unreasonable tribute, since their poverty can
bring him neither honor nor profit. Let him drive all
flatterers and financial schemers out of his court, since
they corrupt the natural goodness of monarchs and
cause trouble between them and their subjects. It is with 90
such people that the punishment of wickedness should
begin. This is the second expedient for maintaining the
peace.

Tolerance is certainly needed in a leader, but in this,
as in everything else, moderation is needed, otherwise it,
too, will be harmful. To be perfectly plain, it is not
tolerance to forgive the wicked; it is cruelty, because
inpunity will make them more daring and will foment
their malice. Archidamedes, seeing that men praised
Charillus, King of Sparta, for his clemency, said: "How
can he be a good prince if he is not the enemy of the
wicked?" He was right. A good man naturally abhors
vice, and this trait is especially laudable in monarchs. We
see its value in the case of Alexander Severus, who hated
thieves so much that he became nauseated at the very
sight of them. Andronicus, Emperor of the East,
although he had other undesirable characteristics, still
was virtuous in the matter of punishing crimes
rigorously. He kept all of his people in the path of duty,
especially governors and officers who were forced to
walk the straight and narrow. As a result, the people had
never been so happy. But the case of Justin II is worth 91

noting. When he saw that the people were suffering outrages at the hands of the great, he resolved to remedy this state of affairs. For this purpose he created a high provost to whom he gave sovereign authority in matters of justice. The new appointee had hardly entered upon the duties of his office when he was told of an injury done by a high-ranking citizen to a poor man. The provost commanded the culprit to appear before him. Since the order was ignored, the provost went right into the palace to seek the criminal out, while he was seated at the emperor's table. In the presence of Justin, the culprit was carried off and tried without any interference or opposition from the emperor. Oh, if only justice were carried out that way, how happy a state would be! How the prince would be loved by his own people and honored by foreigners! Having a kingdom is nothing if justice is not to be found there. If the important officers are not required to do their duty, the kingdom loses its name and becomes a den of thieves. Do we not know that the Holy Roman Emperor lost almost all of his kingdom because of his
92 lieutenants who tyrannized the people? If he had punished them on the strength of the just complaints made, his empire would not be so small as it is now.

Is there any need to name the others who have lost the most beautiful jewels of their crowns because of the insolence of their officers? A prince must keep his eye on the behavior of all of his subjects. However, he is particularly responsible for those to whom he gives important positions. All of their actions, good and bad, are imputed to him. If these men are kept in check, the rest will be easy to manage, for there is no man so wicked or desperate that he does not tremble when he sees a magistrate, a captain, or other persons of high rank punished. The most noble thing a monarch can do is to take the humble people under his protection and keep them safe from the oppression of the great who often abuse their power by using it only to do violence to those weaker than themselves.

As for other petty thieves and murderers, he must also punish them unremittingly. Since they are in the habit of leaving the country after committing their crimes, the monarch needs to act as Mohammed II did
toward Julian de' Medici's assassin who had gone to hide 93
in Constantinople. The Sultan sent him back to Florence bound hand and foot. If this were done, the wicked would be greatly discomfited, realizing that everyone was closing the door to them and that they could find no asylum anywhere. I know that one should not turn strangers away from his door, and that it is to a monarch's credit to receive in a friendly way those who beg his mercy and put themselves under his protection. But this should apply only to merchants or to those who are being wrongly persecuted or harassed. It should not apply to traitors, rabble-rousers, and assassins who disturb the peace and head the list of evil-doers. Such pests are unworthy of compassion. Who would want to have such guests? How could a king be secure if he welcomed all those who had dishonored their own country? I mean here the fomentors of sedition in whose punishment all monarchs have a stake, so much so that they should give them no place of refuge. Otherwise they will bring disaster upon their state and
will give their own subjects reason to make bold plans 94

for a new order of things.

There is certainly no crime so deserving of punishment as sedition, nor is there any against which you need to take so many precautions, for it takes many forms and assumes many different disguises. Sometimes it shows a laughing face which promises liberty and a welcome relief from oppression; sometimes it has only one head, and at other times (and this is the horrible part) you see a hundred thousand of them. We must expose the different faces of evil so that we may more easily do away with it. Either the ambition of a restless chief, or leader, or a general feeling on the part of the people is certainly at the root of all seditious plots.

Any given fomenter of sedition reveals his ambition either directly or indirectly. He does it directly when he tries to take over the state by force. In this case, there are several conditions that can prepare the way for him. Chief among these is the weakness of the ruler. This is what brought disaster upon Childeric, the last of the Merovingians. He is the one whom Pepin, with the
95 consent of the French, had shut up in a monastery. This happened because of Childeric's indifference. Charles the Simple was deposed for the same reason, and his successors were no more fortunate. The remedy of this ill lies in the Prince who is also the cause. If he wins the affections of his people by his goodness, and if he gains their respect by his virtue, then he will be protected against all uprisings. But if he allows the violent passions of greed and anger to get the better of him, he is tempting fate; this will be even more true if he leads a life of ideleness and ease, which will produce contempt on the part of his people. Then foreigners will impose

their will upon him, and his subjects will free themselves and no longer obey him, especially those who have means and authority.

It will be just like what happened to our kings when Charlemagne's race degenerated and France was divided up by ambitious governors. Taking advantage of the simple-mindedness of their masters, they seized control of their provinces. At the same time, some of the Italian lords, for example, the Dukes of Benevento, Friuli, and Spoleto, formed cantons and appropriated the territories where they had been in command. In later
years others followed their example and did the same 96
thing in defiance of the emperors, to their great loss. It is true that the difficulties that they were having in the country where they lived, along with the disgrace the Popes had incurred, prevented them, to a great extent, from putting a stop to the activities of these petty kings.

People of bad temper and easy morals are not easy to hold in check when their leader is not constantly before their eyes. They will seize the first available opportunity to throw off their yoke. The Greeks had a similar experience. Not being able to hold onto Italy themselves, they were forced to abandon it and permit Theodoric, a Goth, to proclaim himself king. After the expulsion of the Lombards, the kings of France and Germany did not manage affairs any better there. They discovered that the Alps were too high for their authority to pass over them, and that if it were blown down there by any wind of fortune, it did not stay long. This serves to confirm the historians' view *that it is harder to keep a province than it was to subjugate it*,
since a conquest requires mere force while retention 97

depends on the prudence and continued good fortune of the victor and true affection on the part of the subjects.

These three things are very rare, particularly the last, of which there is little hope if the prince is far-removed from his people as necessarily happens in a large monarchy whose lands are not all adjacent. It is not easy to love or respect something that one never sees. This is what prompted the Spaniards to offer their kingdom to the Duke of Calabria seeing that their legitimate sovereign, Charles V, was disposed because of his imperial dignity to live in Germany. There was, in my opinion, nothing more instrumental in giving the Flemish and the Dutch the incentive to revolt against Philip II of Spain than the fear of being exposed to the avarice and cruelty of his lieutenants. They considered that such men were accustomed to take liberties when far away from their master, and, in so doing, often thwarted his wishes. This is why the King of Spain
98 allows no viceroy to remain in the Indies more than three years, for he knows that when a man has a taste for power, he easily allows himself to be tempted into usurping authority or rebelling outright.

This is a fact that should surprise no one, for ambition is what makes a son take up arms against his father. Henry, King of England, was attacked by his children at the instigation of his wife, Eleanor. Louis XI caused Charles VII a great deal of trouble. Louis I was treated even worse by his children who deposed him and put him in a monastery. Henry V took the empire away from his father; Andronicus the younger from his grandfather. Adolf imprisoned his father, Arnold, Duke of Gelder[land]. When the Duke of Burgundy tried to

bring about a reconciliation between them by suggesting
a pension of six thousand florins and the title of Duke
which the good old man could retain during his lifetime,
the rest being at the free disposition of Adolf, this
unnatural son said: "*I would prefer to have thrown my
father in a well and jumped in after him than to have
given him this allowance. He has been Duke for
forty-three years; it is high time that I should be. I* 99
*would gladly give him three thousand florins a year, on
condition that he never set foot in the Duchy.*"

Ambition is blind. It respects neither friendship nor blood relationship. Foreseeing this, Prester John keeps all the princes of the blood prisoner in a castle for fear that by their authority they should entice his subjects into some sort of rebellion. This is a barbarous custom, but the Ottoman Turks have an even worse one. They put their brothers to death so that they may reign more freely. A monarch can certainly make his state secure without committing all these cruel acts. On whom can he depend if he should dispose of those closest to him? Would it not be better to gain their affection and give them a stipend in keeping with their rank? In this way he would be following the example of the ancient emperors who used to divide their sovereign domains among their closest heirs and thus removed all discontent.

It would be a strange and monstrous thing to see a
prince attacked by his son or brother to whom he gave 100
so many honors and whom he treated so well. I am well
aware that Louis the Pious is accused of imprudence
because he gave too much to his children, but this is not
the real cause of his misfortune. The principal causes of

the rebellion against him were the little ability that he showed in worldly affairs, the cruel manner in which he treated his nephew Bernard, King of Italy, and the other lords who had attended him, the affection that he lavished on his last son to the neglect of those of his first marriage, and the arrogance of his second wife who disposed of both king and kingdom as she pleased.

In short, against this one example, I could put ten totally different ones, all demonstrating that good blood cannot lie, and that it is less dangerous to a king to maintain a prince of his family than to elevate outsiders. For strangers, having less natural obligation to the sovereign, have less affection for him too. Therefore, it is easier for the desire to reign to push them into trying to overthrow the state whenever they have the means and some likely pretext at hand.

101 Ambitious men commonly conceal their designs under a cloak of zeal and charity. They speak earnestly of the public good and a reformation of the state, but they have nothing of the sort in their hearts. How could it possibly be that the great should want to help the people, since they trample them underfoot and do not hesitate to beat or torment a villager or a townsman as if he were a dog or some beast of burden? To make such injustice appear unimportant, they ridicule the names "bourgeois," "peasant," and "boor." They scorn these men themselves to such an extent that they avoid speaking to them. They are scandalized at meeting one of them, and disguise themselves in all manner of ways so as not to bear the slightest resemblance to those whom they refer to as serfs. They would like to have nothing in common with them. They are annoyed at

having to breathe the same air and at having the same physical features. They would gladly lodge a formal complaint because God gave to everyone equally one sky at which to look and one earth on which to walk. A 102
nation would have to be very stupid to support the ambitions of such persons. Thus the towns do not want to take them in; the peasants flee before them; only malcontents follow them.

Those who have a reputation for piety gain the people's confidence to a much greater extent and can more easily lead them into something new. Witness the hermit, Schacoculis. After having played this role for seven years in the desert where he received visits as a holy man even from the Emperor Bayezid and received gifts from him as well, he finally took off his mask and declared himself the founder of a new sect. He had so many followers that, with their aid, he was able to seize several cities. He defeated a Pasha and the son of Bayezid and would have gone much further, had he not provoked the Sophy. Some time later, a certain Calendar shook the foundations of Anatolia with his false devotion. He kept the Turks on the alert until he was killed in a pitched battle. Was this not the same path that Elmahel the African took to make war on his master, the King of Morocco, in order to deprive him of his scepter and his life?

The respect we have for religion is a very powerful 103
influence on our minds. The moment a man has the reputation of living a saintly life, and especially if he also has the gift of expressing himself eloquently, he can persuade the people to believe anything he wishes. Arrius and Mohammed used such means to found their

doctrine. More recently, what an organization Luther and Calvin have created by using their voices and writings to good effect under the pretext of reforming the abuses of Christianity! Such persons must be restrained and forbidden, on pain of harsh punishment, to preach their dogmas either in public or in private. Such men attract the people, who allow themselves to be influenced too easily by the appearance of piety as well as by the hope of more freedom and a better lot in life.

These are the two spurs that fomenters of faction use on this many-headed animal in order to make him take the field: They show him the tranquility that reigns under democratic equality on the one hand, and the violent actions of the monarchical form of government on the other. This is not a very difficult task, for people do not bear the yoke of princes willingly, especially when these rulers are extortioners or tyrants. Certainly
104 it is true that princes sometimes become hateful and unbearable, but often their subjects too are at fault. They provoke their ruler by attempting a presumptuous rebellion and by seeking unlimited power.

Sovereigns' actions are not supposed to be criticized. If they do wrong, it is up to the One who put them in power to punish them. It is not the responsibility of the people, who owe them complete obedience. Since sovereign rulers are answerable only to God, and since they are His lieutenants, it is presumptuous of men to call them to account. It is a sacrilege to murmur against them or to make attempts on their state or their person. The wisest men are of this opinion, and Christian doctrine specifically exhorts us to revere our Kings and

superiors without distinguishing between the good and the bad. David is a notable example of this. He never wanted to touch his enemy, Saul, an impetuous and tyrannical prince, who had cruelly persecuted him and who, in his hatred of David, had killed Ahimelech and all the priests of Nob, their wives, and their children.
Although on two occasions David had Saul in his power, 105
he felt that it would be wrong for him to injure his enemy despite his hatred for what this man had done. He also prevented others from harming Saul, saying that he would never attack God's annointed.

Is there a king anywhere who tyrannized his subjects as did Nebuchadnezzar? After taking Jerusalem by storm, pillaging the houses and razing the walls, he massacred a large number of the people and led the rest captive to Babylon. Here he had a statue of himself erected which all had to adore or be burned alive. Even so, the prophets of that time cried out against Zedekiah, the King of Jerusalem, for having revolted against his sovereign, and they exhorted the Jews who had been taken to Babylon to pray for the prosperity of this same Nebuchadnezzar and his children. If these reasons do not move us, then history, which is the teacher of imprudent men, has always demonstrated that revolts were useless and that revolutionaries, instead of improving their lot, usually fell out of the frying pan into the fire. What did the Florentines gain by the death of Alessandro de' Medici? How did the inhabitants of
Ghent profit from their revolt against Charles V? 106

One could mention the Swiss and also the Dutch who were fortunate enough to emancipate themselves. As for the Dutch, they owe the existence of their republic to the terrain of their country which is good for defensive purposes, to the alliance with their neighbors, and to the absence of the King of Spain. The republic would indeed be seriously endangered, however, if this king were to turn upon them with all his force. With respect to the Swiss, their unity and skill in arms, coupled with the little wealth they have, discourage any desire to subjugate them and to restore the monarchy which treated them so badly that the rebellion should not really be blamed on them, but on the overbearing governors who dared to lay hands not only on their goods, but also on their persons and their women.

Most peoples do not restrict themselves to such justified self-defense. They revolt because of a tax, because of the advancement of a favorite, or because of a bad administration as if these evils were inherent in monarchy and were not more widespread in
107 democracies where intrigues, corruptions, factions, and crimes committed with impunity are everyday occurrences. In a democratic form of government the best speechmakers do as they please, the virtuous are suspect, the magistrates little respected, the fomenters of sedition promoted; justice is sold to the highest bidder and carelessly administered. This can all be found in the republics of Athens and Rome, the most flourishing ever to have existed. The citizens were always at loggerheads with one another, the rich against the poor, the nobles against the commoners; they even stoned one another in public assemblies. The extent of the massacres, pillaging, and confusion that followed was such that the worst tyranny would not have done half so much evil; and these same people could find no

better remedy than to establish a dictatorship.

In the same way, while they were governing themselves, the Florentines saw nothing but changes and disorder in their city: houses burned, streets paved with corpses, and other tragedies which continued until the monarchy was restored. The Genoese were not much 108
more successful with their liberty and would still be at sword's point if they did not fear their protector. Everyone knows what the protection of a city means to a powerful neighboring prince. If republics have recourse to the authority of a sovereign for protection against destruction, then people who are accustomed to such an arrangement should not depart from it on any pretext or occasion whatsoever.

Tyranny is troublesome, I confess, but public furor and confusion are even worse especially since they have a fixed cause, the mood of the people, who, by nature, are and always will be fickle, ignorant, cruel, and prone to innovation. Tyranny on the other hand disappears with time, and often a wicked prince improves by himself without being forced to do so, as Augustus and Titus did, or else he becomes bored with public affairs, as did Sulla and Diocletian, who abdicated of their own free will. Such persons must be endured just as one suffers a bad year and looks forward to a better one. 109
Since the affairs of the world are always characterized by vicissitudes, evil succeeds good as happiness does adversity; and after the storm of an unjust government, the serenity of a pleasant and peaceful reign shines forth.

If the people took this into consideration, or if they were capable of doing so, they would not rebel for such trivial reasons. But we must admit that men increase their own miseries to a great extent by being too impatient and hypersensitive. No sooner do they experience the slightest difficulty, than they wish to apply a violent remedy. They howl about tyranny but still practice it with impunity in their own homes. Have we not all seen the injustices of masters toward their servants, fathers toward their children, teachers toward their disciples? Abuse of power and arrogance toward inferiors are common vices. I do not say this to excuse bad princes, who cannot be criticized enough, but rather I wish to show that it is better to have a head, even though filled with a cold, than to have none at all.

I wish to show too that tyranny does not release
110 subjects from the obedience they owe to their sovereign, and even less does the dissipation of financial resources or an unjust allotment of salaries do so. In such cases, one must proceed by humble remonstrances and must show the prince the consequences resulting from these abuses and not come armed to demand their reform. This is what people are wont to do, to their own great detriment, for soldiers can do them more damage in six months than a bad government can in ten years. War is no remedy for internal political difficulties, especially one that is undertaken against one's own sovereign. The latter must not give occasion for war, but in order to ensure security, he should always have an armed guard to intimidate rebels, who become daring when they see a prince with too few attendants and not suspicious of anyone.

Julius Caesar was ill-advised to dismiss his guard; Justinian found it best to have his soldiers near him

during the uprising in Byzantium during which the rebels had elected a new emperor, who was killed along with forty thousand inhabitants. We can judge to what extremity Justinian was reduced since he had to 111
slaughter such numbers in his own capital city. If he had not had enough forces to put down the mutineers, he would have been lost just as Cosmo de' Medici would have been in danger of losing his state if he had not courageously opposed the uprisings of the Florentines.

The general public is proud and haughty when faced with someone who cannot resist; a ruler must show his teeth if he wants to be convincing. This is also true of individuals who would stir up the country. They will not be so daring when they see that the sovereign is ready to put down revolts and punish the leaders. Just let him show the rod or the stick, and the greatest will bow to his commands and not dare to offend him. To be even more secure, let him never give absolute power to any other man for fear of having the same thing happen to him that happened to our first kings who were finally driven out by the mayors of the palace whom they allowed to do everything so as to lead a leisurely, retiring life themselves. This is a serious defect 112
in a monarch. As the emperor Vespasian said, a monarch should die with his boots on and not in bed.

While I believe that a monarch needs officers and lieutenants, nevertheless, just as the sun makes the smallest stars shine without diminishing its own light, so he must not delegate authority without retaining the right to the final word and the principal role. If by chance he sees that one of his vassals has already acquired influence, either by his wealth or by his noble birth, he must grant him more honor than power. He should make him a Grand Master, chief of his council, or governor of his capital city. These are offices with little real power but great honor and are worthy of the first princes of the kingdom. The ministries of war and the navy and important governorships are better in the hands of other, lesser lords. It is a principle of political wisdom to give honor to some and power to others. As a result, everyone is happy, and the sovereign is more secure, since he does not need to fear the designs of a humble gentleman as much as those of a powerful and distinguished one.

113 This is why Augustus did not give the governorship of Egypt to senators, fearing that they would seize this rich province that was so important to the Empire. In the same way, the office of Grand Provost, a post in which one could do as much alone as the High Constable, the Grand Master, the Chancellor, and the Captain of the Guard combined, was given only to a knight. Even then it was divided equally between two persons so that they could counterbalance each other and be held in the line of duty by mutual fear. One cannot use too many precautions where there is a danger of sedition. Such resistance to lawful authority must be not only anticipated, but also punished mercilessly.

Now there are other persons who do not attack the public so openly, but who are, nonetheless, extremely dangerous. Drones, quarrelsome persons, spendthrifts, and gamblers, for example, are not thought of as being criminals, but they are not much better. We have already spoken of drones. The quarrelsome have a strong propensity for doing evil; all they want is war,

and when they cannot find public enemies, they seek 114
private ones. This vice is common among the people of the north who are proud and insolent and cannot live without fighting or quarreling with someone. Such behavior must be changed, for one of two things will happen. Either, and this is most frequently the case, they will attack a weak man and heap indignities upon him, then, after they have amused themselves, they will commit a flagrant injustice. If this should happen, respect for the prince and the law will be diminished, and confusion will inevitably result. Or else, they will approach a man of courage, and when they come to blows, if they have any influence, they will draw their relatives and friends into the quarrel, a course that usually has dangerous consequences.

There is only one remedy suitable for this eventuality, that is, to force the parties to the quarrel to give reasonable compensation to those whom they have offended. When I say "reasonable compensation," I mean in proportion to the injury received. A person who has received a beating should get more than someone who has only been slapped or contradicted.
Besides this, an insult to a lord or a magistrate should be 115
punished more severely than one to a cobbler or a porter. The status of the persons involved complicates a given deed and makes it more or less serious. These considerations are left to the discretion of the judges. Frankly, however, these judges take another man's honor too lightly and do not punish insults rigorously enough. An insolent and rash man who has insulted someone will be let off with two or three days imprisonment, and if he should have friends, he will be

out before three hours are up. They will ask only that he apologize and pay the court costs. Still the beating has been given, and the one who was beaten still has to suffer the same of it.

The result has been that men have felt constrained to call out their enemies to save their honor, because they have no other means of redress for their injuries. This is the cause of the duels, so common today, particularly in France, which our kings are trying to prevent. But they will never be able to do it, unless they give orders to award greater satisfaction to persons having sustained
116 injury either to their person or to their honor. It is only right to punish these duellers-to-the-death, to treat them ignominiously after their death, to confiscate their goods, which should be given to charity. But it is more imperative to destroy the source, that is, the arrogance of the attackers. What can a man of honor do when he has been insulted, especially if he is a professional soldier? Shall he go and complain to the judge? He would become a laughing-stock because of the little compensation he would receive. Shall he ask permission to fight a duel? This will be put down to cowardice, all the more so if he were content to accept satisfaction in the presence of five or six persons. Being reduced to such straits, he must either hide forever and never again appear in public, or he must avenge himself by committing murder regardless of the cost.

If, on the other hand, he could hope to receive sufficient satisfaction to vindicate his honor, he would not resort so readily to force. An insult would be
117 punished by a reprimand, while bodily harm would be repaid in kind. While the law of equal punishment,

which the Latins called Talio, seems to be suitable here, I should advise, nevertheless, going even further and punishing every offense doubly, since, in the execution of such a law, difficulties often arise. That is, for every blow or lash given, the offender would receive two, publicly and in the presence of the offended party. As for words or biting sarcasm, the offender should be forced to make honorable amends according to the merits of the case and the status of the persons offended. I say "biting sarcasm" since there are so many different kinds. While one should not take offense at every little thing, still there are many ways of being offensive. Often a gesture or a contemptuous expression rankles in a noble heart more than a violent act would.

Is it not clear that most quarrels start with presumptuous utterances on the part of someone who cannot say a word without offending someone else? No
restraint is too strong to use on such insolence. As for 118
those who lay violent hands on another, I am of the opinion that they should receive double what they gave, which is not at all unreasonable. Roman law forced a robber to repay four times over. Why should we not punish just as rigorously those who violate another's honor, which is much more precious than one's goods or one's life? Why should we put up with a drone (most quarrelsome people belong to this category) who elbows his way into a group, and not knowing what else to do, attacks one person after another? If anyone dares to retaliate, he immediately finds himself being bombarded, and the stronger tramples the weaker. This is done as boldly in the middle of a city as if it were in the corner of some wood. Is there any hope for peace

when such rabble is permitted to remain unrestrained and to sap the foundations of public tranquility? They must be treated in the same way that they treat others. Since they so boldly attack another man's honor, they should be punished ignominiously. It would be a good idea to put them in the stocks for a day; they would be
119 as usefully employed there as they ever are, and there would be fewer contradictions for a yes or a no. Everyone would be more careful of his words and his actions.

Someone is going to say that to scrutinize so closely every word and gesture is too severe. I would answer that this severity is necessary, and that all behavior that undermines the state is punishable. Society has no use for quarrellers, dare-devils, or cutthroats. Princes will get along very well without them too and ought to exterminate them. Otherwise they will never get rid of the assassinations and duels that will decimate their monarchy. If the above-mentioned suggestions are followed, no one will be anxious to offend or insult another, and thus the cause of these misfortunes will be removed. There is no man so vindictive that he will not be satisfied if he sees his enemy publicly beaten or receiving a reprimand more shameful than the insult he himself suffered. Then it will be only right to punish dueling with extreme rigor, to bring infamy upon those who quibble about a point of honor and are so
120 hypersensitive that they refuse an honorable settlement that would give them back their honor unsullied and would allow them to enjoy the spectacle of the shame and ignominy of their adversary.

Someone may object that the injured party cannot

always prove that he has been insulted, and, therefore, the law not being able to give him satisfaction for lack of proof, he will still be forced to call his man out for a duel. This is indeed an important point. Because of it the ancient Franks, Lombards, and other Germanic tribes permitted duels, and asking for them was an honorable act. (Today these formalities are less important. One simply sends out a challenge with utter disregard for the prince, who is master of his subjects' lives, and who should not allow them to be squandered without his permission.) Therefore, he should not forbid duels entirely when the offended party does not have sufficient evidence of the wrong that he said he received and when there is sufficient reason to believe that what he says may be true. This is to prevent the assassinations and factions that might follow if such permission were denied.

Often two men are so set upon destroying each other 121
that it is impossible to reconcile them, and what is worse, if they are rich and powerful, they cause factions to arise in a city or kingdom. In such a case, it is expedient to have them fight it out between themselves so that their blood can quench any fires of civil disunity that may be ignited. There is only one way to avoid having to go to such extremes, that is, to ward off quarrels by an ignominious punishment, as we have said. Some would perhaps prefer to issue a challenge rather than to ask for legal satisfaction when they have been repudiated or otherwise affronted. But when they see their enemies so harshly punished for slanderous speech, and when, moreover, they consider the disgrace brought upon those who fight duels without the prince's

permission, I think that they will exercise some restraint and will accept a settlement that is no less honorable than certain. The fear of a shameful punishment ought to encourage them to make this decision, so that those who seek honor in duels will find nothing but dishonor for themselves and their children.

122 This is an uncivilized custom that was never practiced among the most famous nations, except in time of war. On these occasions a man offered to fight for the honor of his country, or two enemy nations, in order to avoid a great outpouring of blood, agreed to let the decision of their quarrel rest on the outcome of an individual combat among two or three champions. These men were chosen by each side on the condition that their victory would redound to their countrymen who would impose their will on the defeated. Thus the differences between the Romans and the Albans was ended by the combat of the three Curiaces and the three Horaces. Inasmuch as those who fought for the Romans won, the Albans immediately put down their arms and surrendered to their enemies according to the agreement.

I have never found in any history book a quarrel that was more honorably ended than the one between Varenus and Pulfio. These two soldiers in Caesar's army were always quarrelling with each other and could not be reconciled until one day when, being very close to the enemy, Pulfio had the idea of saying to Varenus:
123 "What better occasion could we find, Varenus, to show our courage? This is the hour when all will see which of us is the more skilful man." After saying this, he threw himself headlong among the enemy squadrons and killed many of them, but in the end he was surrounded by a

great multitude who bore him to the ground. Upon seeing this, Varenus, afraid that he might be considered a coward, ran boldly forward to help his companion. When the enemy saw him, they left Pulfio and turned upon him. Pulfio, who had been rescued by his old adversary, did not leave him in this moment of need. To repay him in kind, Varenus defended him against the enemy and saved him from certain doom. As a result, they were reconciled and were honored and applauded by the whole army. If, following the example of these two soldiers, those who have some quarrel to settle between themselves were to prove their valor against a common enemy, they would be considered more worthy of praise.

Today, however, the rules of virtue and magnanimity 124
have become perverted. We stake our honor on meaningless little acts of bravery that the ancients scorned. Even the Turks make fun of duels and attribute them to simple-mindedness or nonsense. In return we dare to call them barbarians, as if there were anything more barbarous than fighting among fellow countrymen, friends, or relatives, and then nursing lasting grudges against them. World peace will remedy this evil if we can only bring it about. If public acts of hostility are forbidden, there is a good chance that private hatred will cease or be diminished.

When this stage has been reached, it will be necessary to regulate everyone's expenditures so that he will not waste his goods. This is a matter of no little importance in the preservation of a state, for when wasters become needy, as will inevitably happen, they will look for opportunities to recoup their losses at someone else's

expense, in order to continue their accustomed excesses. If there is any kind of disturbance in the offing, these
125 people are always the first to lend their support to it. Cataline had hardly any supporters besides those who had wasted their fortunes in taverns, brothels, and gambling houses. Taverns are only for travelers. Brothels are tolerated in some countries to avoid a greater evil. But still there would be no need for them if the Roman policy were in force.

The Romans encouraged their citizens to marry by granting them many desirable privileges. Not that I wish to condemn celibacy for priests and monks, but it would be expedient to force the rest of the people to take wives. The Chinese have provided an example. They give their children a vocation and give them in marriage while they are still young for fear that they should become debauched. Added to this is the principle that marriages are the foundation of an empire. But the fact remains that the more one can prevent debauchery the better. It is the first step toward adultery, and it is bad enough that we must put up with sins when they are hidden without actually allowing shops to be set up for them. This is why these infamous places must be outlawed. Here is where the young lose
126 both their bodies and their wealth. In this respect they are worse than gambling houses, which swallow up only money.

Still the ancients, foreseeing the harm that could come of it, did not permit real gambling, nor any kind of wager except on honest games, like wrestling, discus throwing, foot races, or other similar games involving bodily exercise. They rejected entirely all games of chance, so common today in Europe that neither the great nor the humble, neither men nor women, can find any better pastime than to risk, at one throw of the dice, the best part of their fortune, and, at times, all of it.

Some have ruined themselves giving banquets at which the overabundance of food is offered indiscriminately to anyone who comes. The Romans, on the other hand, formulated some rules and limited the expenditure made for a banquet and the number of
guests invited. It is true that no one adhered very closely 127
to this policy, as, in fact, it seems impossible to do. One does not go to another man's house to see what he is eating or to count the guests at his table. Inasmuch, however, as domestic affairs, and especially banquets and gambling, are not so secret that they do not come to light eventually, it would be the duty of the magistrate to expose cases of mismanagement. Who would not judge a man worthy of punishment who was so greedy as to pay four hundred francs for a sea mullet, as did Asinius Celer? Who would not be ashamed to see the son of a mountebank Aesop swallow in a single glass fifty thousand francs worth of pearls dissolved in vinegar? Who would not loathe the gluttony of that wicked Apicius who squandered nearly two million *écus*, and seeing that he had only five hundred thousand francs left, poisoned himself, for fear of starving to death?

The earth should swallow up those monsters who thus abuse its riches. Now this would be a small matter if they ruined only themselves, but we can see that they
also involve their creditors to whom they usually make 128

an assignment. They borrow on all hands and easily find credit because of the impression of wealth and liberality that they give. Then poverty, the daughter of luxury, enters their house and suddenly causes them to go bankrupt. Those who renege on their payments should be given to their creditors as slaves, following the ancient custom still practiced in Ethiopia and the Indies. There would be fewer cheaters, assignees, and rascals around. Everyone would keep a closer watch on his expenditures, not just on food, but also on clothes, too many of which has likewise impoverished many families.

To correct this state of affairs, edicts have been published in France, but they have been to absolutely no avail. Officers of the law do not dare enforce them against the nobility who are the principal offenders, thus doing harm to the sovereign who should either not publish ordonances at all or should see that they are better enforced. He should begin to reform such abuses
129 by making his own servants comply with his edict.
There is no better way of bringing the people into line than this, for they naturally follow the examples set by the court. Let the lords stop wearing satin and velvet; the bourgeois will immediately stop using these materials, without waiting for any direction. But as long as he sees the shining gold and silver on the nobles' dress, he will mortgage all his goods rather than not wear any himself. I know that many people do not run this kind of danger. It is not to them that I am addressing myself. It is particularly to those in our part of the world, the French, the Spanish, and the English, who make a virtue of luxury and consider a man very common if he and his wife do not wear enough gold and

jewels to buy a province. If censure, about which we shall speak a little later, were re-established, it would be appropriate to find out about the life of these ostentatious people. It would be worth knowing where they got their fine possessions and whether they have the means to keep them up.

Still, an example set by the sovereign is the shortest
path to the correction of such abuses; for they are more 130
harmful than people think, since they bring on a general corruption of morals, or at least they are a reflection of it. You see few men who, like Caesar's soldiers, can fight effectively when perfumed, or who, like Aristippus, are incorruptible in the midst of the carousing of the Bacchanalia. Affected bodily ornaments reveal an effeminate personality that places little value on virtuous acts. It is clear then that those given to luxury are more apt to indulge in all kinds of evil; and, for this reason, it must be prevented or punished like any contagious vice capable of leading to others. I shall not elaborate here on heinous crimes like magic, adultery, blasphemy, and atheism, for they are less overt and less frequently found. Of course they must be punished according to the customs of the country. I have chosen to dwell only on the more common and really scandalous crimes that must of necessity be punished if a state is going to continue to exist.

Now we must consider the reward of virtue, which is
of no less importance. Reward and punishment are the 131
two means of maintaining a republic and the two principal effects of distributive justice. The severity of the sentences prevents crimes from increasing disproportionately, and rewards encourage men to do

good. Men who have done something beneficial for the prince or the public deserve to be rewarded. It is certainly reasonable that they should receive some recognition; to do otherwise would show a lack of gratitude. Besides, it is a mistake to forget men of virtue and industry, for these are the qualities that place them above the common herd and make them able to accomplish great things.

Now there are two kinds of reward: profit and honor. Frequently they are found in conjunction with each other, as in estates, offices, and commissions which bring both honor and material gain. A monarch must distribute both of these rewards liberally to deserving persons. This is not often done because it is difficult to see the prince personally. Thus he knows only his servants and those who are recommended to him by his favorites. The favorites make friends at the prince's expense and make him so inaccessible that no one can
132 reach him except through them. Titus said that no man should leave the presence of a prince dissatisfied. Things are very different today, for there is usually sufficient reason to be unhappy before ever speaking to the prince. Certainly a king would offend against his majesty if he were on familiar terms with everyone indiscriminately, but he should not make himself inaccessible to those who have rendered him some notable service, or who might do so in the future. He ought to grant the former a suitable pension and the latter the hope of having one when they earn it.

In short, it is important that he know his subjects himself so that he can judge which ones are able to serve him, and so that he will be aware of the many things his

servants hide from him. If he does this, he will rid the state of a great potential danger, namely, the discontent felt by a man who sees himself removed from the prince's favor when he thinks himself entitled to it because of his rank or service. It is very true that a
king's favor cannot be equally divided. Thus my 133
proposal will not result in the restriction of his natural affections or inclinations. I contend only that he should not deny his benevolence to those who are worthy of it and that the more he can make such persons obligated to him, the better. A monarch needs many friends whom he can neither acquire nor keep unless his generosity is both honest and suited to the recipient. To the end that his gifts be wisely used, it would be expedient, since he cannot know all good men, to have, as did the ancient emperors, a special secretary charged with bringing to his attention those persons who are capable of serving him in some capacity or who have acquitted themselves well in the past. Thus informed, he can give them, on the advice of his council, important governorships or honorable posts.

Because graft is rampant everywhere, no one,
regardless of his capabilities, will ever attain a position 134
of public dignity today unless he has money. Wars have caused this to happen, for they have reduced princes to offering for sale what should be rewards for virtue. When wars have ceased, there will be other, more legitimate means of raising the money necessary for the public treasury. There will be no need to give pensions to foreigners, to maintain so many garrisons and army reservists. When princes have eliminated these superfluous expenditures, and when their houses are in

order, they will no longer have any good reason to sell public offices, nor to permit a traffic in temporal, spiritual, and judicial positions. This has been at the root of all disorders. This is why Alexander Severus declared that he would not put up with office-sellers, because anyone who buys must sell.

I shall not enter into the question of whether or not
offices should be perpetual. This has been debated, and
both sides have put forth reasons with which I am
unconcerned provided that honors be given to virtuous
men regardless of their financial status or their race.
135 These considerations are unimportant unless accom-
panied by virtue, in which case they are worthy of some
prerogative. The Romans understood this very well. (I
mention these people rather frequently, because they
can furnish us with good examples on many issues.)
They chose, in accordance with Pompeian law, the
richest citizens as judges. And, moreover, it was not
possible to become a knight unless an individual had
twenty thousand francs, or a senator unless he had twice
that amount. With this system they did not sell offices,
and they avoided graft which is more apt to tempt a
poor man than a rich one.

The nobility of a family also merits some
consideration, and it is presumed that the son of a good
father will inherit his virtues and will fear incurring
public censure if he has any sensitivity at all. Therefore,
he must be preferred to someone whose ancestors are
unknown, in the event that the two men are equal in
ability and integrity. Still, virtue must always be the
primary consideration in matters of honor and reward,
136 otherwise affairs will never run smoothly. While it may

seem difficult for a monarch to refuse a brother or a mother who presents someone for some position or benefice, still, such recommendations should never be made in the first place unless they are based on the worth of the person presented.

If the monarch should be partial to certain individuals, as does happen, at least let his gifts have some relation to the true worth of the recipient, so that the monarch's generosity does not cause discontent among those whose services are essential to him. Let him consider that one must pay his debts before giving gifts, and that there is no more legitimate debt than a just reward for virtue, which lies chiefly in bestowing high office and honors. The emperor Severus made such a ceremony out of this that he published an official proclamation naming those whom he wished to honor with some commission or governorship. He exhorted the people to bring accusations against any of them if, by chance, they should prove unworthy. There was one condition, however: anyone accusing another falsely should be put to death. He had learned this from the Athenians who inquired into the lives of all their
magistrates and established a special group of registrars 137
for this purpose. Now when we have examined the character of each one, we will give him a position in keeping with his abilities. If he is strong and valiant, we will award him military commands and positions. If he is prudent and politic, we will make him a state councilor. If he is a man of integrity and incorruptible, we will make him a judge. We will grant him the management of finances if he is not greedy, ecclesiastical dignities if he is pious and devout. Thus

everyone will be happy. The prince will be served in a way that will guarantee his honor and the people's best interests. His subjects will have no occasion to murmur, since the state will be well-managed and justice ably administered.

So that the realm may have not only good men but also capable ones at its disposal, industry must be stimulated, and some suitable reward must be given those who excel in the arts and sciences. Those who scorn intellectual and learned men are either barbaric or stupid. Many do this out of spite because they themselves have inferior minds and would like all men
138 to be ignorant so that they may conceal their shame among those like them. Learning is second only to virtue. Again, I am not including here under virtue that common valor of which men make such a display. God forbid that I should place less value on divine perfection than on brute courage which only assumes a mask of virtue and whose only end is pillaging and murder. The greatest princes have always respected the learned and have given or offered them very honorable positions. In the reign of the emperor Commodus, professors of philosophy had an annual salary of six hundred Roman *ecus*, or the equivalent of three thousand francs in our money. Under Marcus Aurelius, the rhetoricians had ten thousand drachmas (that is, more than two thousand pounds). Vespasian had previously given them five thousand francs. But this is nothing in comparison with the generosity of Constantius [Chlorus] who gave the rhetorician Eumenius as much as thirty thousand
139 pounds. I believe that the King of England would have given no less to our own Budé, if the King of France had

not been jealous, and rightfully so, of a person so learned in the Latin and Greek languages.

What shall I say of Caesar, Charlemagne, and so many others who sought to make their names immortal through their writings as well as their armed conquests? No one must suppose that learning weakens a man's courage and takes away his skill in arms, as the Scythians used to think. When they had taken Athens, they wanted to set fire to all the libraries found in the city, but one among them prevented this from happening. This person claimed that they ought to leave the Greeks their books, so that, by spending their time reading, they would lose their valor and thereby become more effeminate and thus more easily ruled. The Goths were of the same opinion. They did not want their kings to have any training in the *belles lettres.* They proceeded on the basis of this illusion and found out, to their sorrow, that the most unlettered and
unenlightened are not the most valiant. They were 140
beaten and driven out like serfs from all of their territories by those very people whom they had scorned. Their reign passed and had so little permanent effect that today we can find hardly a trace of it, except the marks of barbaric rule.

The Athenian and Roman states were much more solid. They combined the exercise of the mind with that of the body with the result that there has never been a more valiant, happy, or wise people. Yet, why do we need to look to antiquity for an example, since we see that in our century the most warlike nations of Europe hold letters in high esteem? I would mention them by name if I were not afraid of scandalizing the others.

Now I believe that theoretical studies are more highly thought of than the mechanical arts. Still, the latter should not be scorned, for work done with the hands is necessary to mankind. Therefore those who excel in it deserve their share of public rewards. Mithridates ordered prizes to be given to the best drinkers. Xerxes gave them to those who invented some new form of
141 sensual pleasure. Actors received a salary for amusing the people.

Is there not all the more reason to honor artisans, and especially those who discover some new and useful invention? We must not be like Tiberius who put a man to death because he had found a way to make glass malleable. Such acts discourage industry. We must certainly not imitate the Ephesians who could not bear to have anyone be outstanding. This is why Heraclitus said that they all deserved to be hanged. Who will not consider the men who invented clocks and printing deserving of a royal pension? Who will not revere the memory of that good Neapolitan who, four hundred years ago, invented the mariner's compass? I am passing over a thousand other inventions that we would not have if their inventors had been so cruelly treated. It is certainly important to have good inventors, especially in architecture, the goldsmith's craft, the arts of navigation and smithery, and similar trades without which we could not get along. A monarch's gifts would not be
142 wasted here. If his revenues are not sufficient to recompense all the men of virtue and industry, at least let him give something to those who excel in these two qualities.

Alleging poverty would be a shameful excuse, though,

especially in time of peace when he has so few expenses that he should have enough to give a little largesse to his servants as well as to other deserving persons. In this, as in other matters, prudence should be his guide; he should consider carefully the resources at his disposal, the amount he can afford to give, and the persons deserving of receiving recognition. He must not give indiscriminately to everyone, as did Heliogabalus who bestowed gifts upon ruffians and procurers. He must make his generosity conform to his means so as not to fall into poverty and destitution, as Caligula and Nero did. The wise king will take his needs into consideration first and will deduct from his income what he must have for the honest maintenance of his court. Then from the remainder he will distribute largesse, judging each man's reward by his condition. Thus, recognizing that a man is industrious, he will award him a suitable pension if he is
poor and will give him honors if he is rich or noble. 143
Honor is the most welcome recompense one can give such people, who place more value on it than on any worldly goods. It is therefore the greatest incentive imaginable for encouraging virtue.

The hope of receiving honor, in ancient times, was what made so many good soldiers out of the Greeks and the Italians. The Olympic games were started for this very purpose, for the victor was given only a simple laurel wreath as a prize. Philip of Macedon was amazed that the Greeks would strive for such an insignificant thing, but he failed to recognize the inestimable honor they received. The winners were formally praised and taken back to their countries by a group of admirers to the accompaniment of applause and joyful songs, not to

mention the statues erected in their honor. In Rome, a triumphal procession was arranged for the same purpose: to give recognition to army generals who had won an outstanding victory. No doubt the hope of such tribute taught them to scorn any thought for their own lives and to expend all their energies freely in the service
144 of the republic. What would a man not do in order to
enter his city amidst such pomp? What would he not undertake to have the honor of knighting a king and giving him his sword, as Captain Bayard did?

Speaking of more peaceable occupations, would there not be more orators if they governed the people, as Demosthenes and Cicero did in ancient times? How many poets there would be if they received a crown from the emperor's hand, as happened at the poetry festivals held on Mount Alba! This was honor with no profit, yet contestants crowded in to vie for it. This is what induced many princes in Europe to institute orders of knighthood. In this way, without any expense to themselves, they can put the best men in their kingdom in their debt. The title "knight," although purely honorary, is nevertheless coveted by a noble man since he thus becomes a brother and companion to his king. There are other honors of less distinction, like the dignity of the office of state councilor, privileges, exemptions from taxes and other fees, that the prince
145 can grant without greatly diminishing his treasuries.

Emperors who made a business of subjugating the world rewarded their followers liberally at the expense of the conquered provinces. They drove out the former owners and awarded the best lands to their captains and soldiers so as to satisfy them and obligate them for continued service in case of future need. Therein, I believe, lies the origin of fiefs, which are nothing but certain lands assigned to someone in recognition of his merits with the stipulation that he respect the donor and attend him in time of war. These grants were held only for life until the time of the emperor Alexander, who made them hereditary in order to favor the children of his men-at-arms who lived like nobles. They were much the same as Duchies and similar honorary estates granted for life to the recipient by our first kings. They were finally made perpetual and became hereditary by the permission or consent of those who have reigned since.

The Sultan has retained the old custom concerning 146
fiefs, for he gives his timars only for life. These lands are conquered territories which he distributes as the Romans did to the most faithful and valiant of his soldiers. The one condition is that they serve him at their own expense in case he should need them. It is said that in the Persian War, forty years ago, he conquered so much land that he created four thousand timars out of it.

But, since conquests seem to be at an end today, which is a tacit warning to princes to come to an agreement on a general peace and to be content with their fortune, other means must be found to finance public largesse. We have already mentioned briefly some means of accomplishing this. Among others, we have spoken in passing of ecclesiastical benefices, a means peculiar to Christian princes of exercising their generosity without loss to their own domains. Thus, they have become accustomed to using them to reward

their good servants and vassals. Even the kings of France used to give abbeys to their princes and gentlemen of high rank. The recipients not only enjoyed the income from such benefices, as they still do today, but also bore
147 the title and were not at all hesitant to call themselves "abbott," even though they were laymen and men-at-arms. This practice existed from the reign of Charles the Bald to that of Robert. The church's wealth is indeed great. What is more, it is unequally distributed, for some have more than their condition requires, others do not have enough, and some, despite their obvious worth, have nothing at all. This abuse has come down to us from the distant past and cannot be eliminated in a day, any more than can many other inequities in the state.

It is therefore expedient to leave the world as it is and permit the holders of these benefices to enjoy their present wealth in peace. But, since they hold only a life interest in them, it is possible, upon their deaths, to make a regulation that would correct this situation. This method would in no way offend them. Is it reasonable
148 that one man should hold a benefice easily capable of supporting four or five men of the same rank? Besides, even a man who holds a rich bishopric is not satisfied unless he can add the revenue of several priories and abbeys to it. All the while, there are innumerable worthy gentlemen, soldiers, and others of different vocations, who are crushed under the most abject poverty, to whom the prince could give an honest appointment. This could be done if the benefices were distributed as they ought to be and not held by such a small number of persons. However, there is a need for a

dual policy in this matter.

The first thing would be to limit the revenue of each
bishopric, abbey, priory, and rectorship and, after
having examined the responsibility and profits of the
said benefices, to assign to the title holders as many
lands or as much income as is judged sufficient to
maintain them honestly. This decision should be made
keeping in mind the appointees' rank, the financial
needs for the maintenance of the divine service, and the
other small expenses customarily paid by the holders.
The remainder could be used to recompense those 149
worthy persons who have served the king or the public
well and who have received either no reward at all or a
very minimal one.

The second policy would be that no one be allowed
to hold two benefices unless one of them should have
insufficient revenue, and unless the holder be of
exceptionally high rank. It is a scandal to see an
insignificant person holding several benefices that he has
solicited, pursued, bartered, pestered someone to get, or
that are acquired by other means no more praiseworthy
than legitimate. Large revenues bring on ambition and
luxury, vices most unsuited to a clergyman who ought
to espouse simplicity and modesty. He has no need to
keep either greyhounds or falcons. It is no part of his
business to be a hunter. He has no need whatsoever for
stables filled with barbary horses, geldings, and Spanish
jennets, since arms are not his profession. Let him be
satisfied with a revenue commensurate with his station
in life; he has no legitimate complaint if the state takes
excess monies and applies them to so charitable and
useful a work as nourishing his deserving but less 150

fortunate compatriots.

This type of act would result in others being moved to follow the example of those who had done good. The people would not have to bear the crushing burden of taxes which the prince is forced to levy in order to underwrite his current expenses and to fill his coffers which are continuously being emptied because no such policy exists. Some will find it strange to take away from men of the church to give to laymen. I should not advise it if the laymen did not need it, and if the clergy did not abuse their riches. But the just dissatisfaction of the one group and the excessive luxury of the other are clearly visible. While I do not approve of the equal division of property as formerly practiced in Lacedaemonia and Rome, still it seems wrong to me to see benefices so unequally distributed when they were founded and enriched by the generosity of good people for the maintenance of the priest and the poor. For this reason, the lands and the revenues that they bring in should be awarded to these two groups.

151 Now among the poor, the ones most deserving of compassion are those who have put the public in their debt by some laudable act for which they have received no recompense. Therefore when such men present themselves to the prince, he will be able to reward them by following the above policy. His first duty, nevertheless, shall be to examine their claims with his best counselors in an effort to weed out those presumptuous persons who, on the pretext of knowing someone at court, pursue appointments to which they are not entitled. It is wise for the prince to hear the humble supplications of his subjects and to receive their

requests, but, before granting them, it is judicious for him to take up the matter with his council. Otherwise, forward men will receive what was intended for the virtuous, and, taking advantage of the readiness of the prince, will beg for his favors through intermediaries. These, in turn, are most irresponsible for they have recommended straw men. But they are the cause of still
another wrong: they take all the credit for the kindness 152
and generosity of the prince. He himself can correct this abuse if he has every man whom he wishes to reward called personally into his presence and also if he refers him, as I have mentioned, to his council. No one will dare to make improper requests, if he sees that the prince grants nothing frivolously, and that he will not act except on the advice of his good officers.

In order to administer these affairs properly he needs two registers. One will contain an abstract of his financial affairs and a record of his ordinary expenses, the other a list of his officers and domestics with the appointments and gifts that they and their relatives have received. The first will show what he is able to give, the second will tell him whom he has already rewarded either financially or with offices. He will then dismiss them courteously when they ask him for another gift. By so doing he will be sure to share his favors with those who have not yet received anything. The kings of Persia had such a register, witness Ahasuerus. After leafing through his register and discovering that he had never given any
recognition to the outstanding services of Mordecai, he 153
overwhelmed him with as much kindness and honor as a man could wish. Because of the great number of affairs that pass through the monarch's hands, he often forgets

the services of his subjects. Consequently, he does not give them anything if, by chance, they are of a modest disposition and are ashamed to ask. On the other hand, he gives too much to the ones who are bold and importunate. These men obtain the best benefices and grants through the offices of their agents despite the fact that they do not deserve anything.

All this causes a great deal of discontent. When Basil the Macedonian succeeded to the empire, he found that the treasury had been exhausted by such persons, so much so that the first thing he did was to have them make restitution of half of what they had unjustly received. However, because it is difficult to reclaim what has been given, it is better to check with the council before giving the gifts, and, following the example of Charles VIII, the monarch should declare all gifts of a considerable size null and void if they are not approved.
154 It goes without saying that it is impossible to regulate the expenditures of a monarch, since it is sometimes appropriate to give presents that must be kept secret. These may be given either to subjects or to foreigners. If he gives to subjects, they can expect to have the gifts approved later if they are deserving. If they are not, then they ought to be patient and be satisfied with some small reward which is completely at the discretion of the prince, for he should not ask the advice of his council on petty matters. In order to avoid this situation, Charles VII declared by express edict the sum that he wished to have at his disposal each year to use at his discretion. As for foreigners, if they are assigned a pension, or if they are secretly given a gift, it is in time of war or danger of war in order to persuade them to

betray their masters and give away their secrets. This
will no longer be done in time of world peace, when
there will be no out but ambassadors to receive gifts.
But even if this liberality is public, honest, and
moderate, it will still be unnecessary because of the
general assembly of which we have spoken. In short, a 155
monarch's finances cannot be too carefully guarded
since the preservation of his state and the well-being of
his people depend on them.

A ruler's subjects always bear the brunt of his immoderate liberality. His generosity would be much more effective if employed to alleviate the distress of the poor, who are growing in number at too rapid a rate. If care is not taken, they will be capable of undermining states, as the slaves did once in Italy. There is nothing that makes a man more desperate than hunger and privations. There have always been poor people, and they are very necessary, for the balance that exists in republics depends, in part, on the inequality of possessions. Still, these people must be pitied, especially the crippled, blind, old, sick, and weak. As for those who are healthy and fit, they too must be fed, and, if they are young, taught a trade so that they will be able to earn their own living.

If, however, they are old enough and strong enough,
they can be of some service. Princes and cities always
need laborers and workmen to erect buildings, pave
roads, caulk ships, and repair walls, bridges, and 156
fortresses. The first Caesars undertook to erect great
buildings which were not always really necessary, but
they wanted to add beauty to their empire and to
support the many poor people who would otherwise

have starved to death. The Venitians today nourish, in the Arsenal, two or three thousand persons, knowing full well that it is a work of charity to use public money to benefit the poor by giving them work. To this end too, well-managed cities have homes where they keep needy people who are not ill; they become supply centers of new artisans and discourage vagabonds and drones who are just looking for the opportunity to beg and steal. There are some among the poor who should not be shut up or treated like the others, namely, those who have been ruined by wars, fire, and like accidents, and who are ashamed to beg. They would be more suitable recipients of alms than those master-beggars who have never had any other trade. Actually, it is
157 easier to prevent poverty in the first place than to remedy it after it has taken hold. Since experience teaches us that wars, lawsuits, and taxes are what send men to the poorhouse, let us remove these causes, and we shall no longer see so many wretched beggars.

The first cause is the most important, and the other two are contingent on it, for in time of war the common people are burdened down with taxes. In the countryside they are pillaged by soldiers and in the towns by userers to whom in their need they are forced to have recourse. From all of this result lawsuits, which complete the ruin of many families. Thus, world peace is a good means of preventing these misfortunes. It will give the laborer back his fields and his freedom; it will rid him of the increased taxes levied in time of war; finally, it will free him from the tyranny of userers whose fortunes are built on another's ruin. His only remaining worry will be lawsuits form which even peace

cannot protect him completely. It takes only one bad
neighbor, a vindictive, ill-tempered person, to involve a
peaceable man in a lawsuit and cause him to spend his
fortune on chicanery. Added to this is the fact that 158
some people find their only pleasure in such suits.
Witness that Parisian merchant who was never willing to
stop his lawsuits, even though Francis I personally asked
him to do so and promised to seek a profitable
compromise for him with all the opposing parties,
debtors, and creditors. Such litigants ought to be
punished, at least financially, as the Greeks and Romans
did. They made a solemn pledge and set aside a certain
sum from both parties to a suit until the case was
decided, whereupon the money of the loser was
forfeited. Today such fines have no place except in cases
in the appelate court, and even then they are so small
that hardened litigants pay no attention to them. In
Greece they amounted to a tenth of the amount being
contested in civil cases and a fifth in criminal cases.

Now this injustice arises principally from the men
who practice law. On the pretext of defending their
clients, they industriously drag out the suits and seek to 159
make them into immortal precedents, since this is their
one aim in life. There is no fact so crystal clear that they
cannot make it doubtful. There is no case so obvious
that they cannot make it seem confusing, no statute
whose execution they cannot stay by malicious
subtlety. This is what made Cato say that the law courts
should be paved with traps. If judges identify with such
persons, or if they allow themselves to be caught
off-guard by them, what hope is there for seeing justice
well administered? What is a poor litigant to do when he

sees postponement after postponement of his case when it could have been terminated so promptly? Where will he find the courage to serve his prince and to respect the magistrates, when he sees all his money used up to pay legal fees before he can obtain justice?

There have been several policies in France aimed at correcting this situation, the most useful and laudable being the abolition of the office of prosecuting attorney. Our ancestors foresaw that to allow a profession whose very existence depended on the initiation and continuance of lawsuits would ultimately lead to the same position as that of the Athenian judges;
160 they put off cases as long as a hundred years, since men do not try to end something that is profitable to them. Thus, our forefathers forbade any speeches by the prosecutors except in case of need. Even then a proxy had to be obtained from the prince. This proxy expired with the Parliament, thus no one could be assured of living at the expense of the litigants. Moreover, they made everyone plead his case in turn. All could then be sure of being heard in the order in which they had come before the court to ask for justice. Nor were the presiding judges allowed to grant extraordinary audiences except on Thursdays. To keep judges of the lower courts in line, it was the usual custom for appellants to sue them for denial of justice and make them adjourn their court so that they could come to the appelate court and answer for their sentences at the risk of their lives and fortunes.

These rules are good if only they were followed. Basil the Macedonian found other ways to solve these problems. First, he paid a certain sum to those who did

not have the means for appealing to justice for their
rights. Secondly, because there was so much confusion 161
caused by the multiplicity and obscurity of the laws, which everyone interpreted to suit himself, he decided to do away with all the useless and ambiguous ones. Then he placed on the bench judges of irreproachable honesty and paid them good wages. He enjoined them to sit all day and to settle the suits with all possible equity and diligence. Finally, he took the trouble to become acquainted with the differences and complaints that arose among the people. He never failed to do this unless war or consultations with his ambassadors prevented it. It even happened that one day, having come to the courts and seeing that no one approached him, he sent out into the city of Constantinople to inquire whether or not anyone had any complaints to make. When he was informed that everyone was happy, he wept with joy and gave thanks to God.

These were all acts of a great monarch, who ought to dispense justice to his subjects, the humble as well as the great, the peasants as well as the nobles. This in no way
diminishes his greatness. His name alone will protect 162
him from scorn. The best things are shared by all. The sun sends its rays equally on gold and on mud. Water flows in public domain. God preserves the lives of the smallest animals. Why then should a king keep himself from his people? Why should he not keep in close touch with his subjects. He can then receive their requests directly, hear about their sufferings from their own lips. The misery of the people is ordinarily suppressed or disguised through the connivance of his favorites and domestics whose only concern is an easy life for

themselves and who care no more about a peasant or a townsman than they do about a dumb beast.

Augustus, Claudius, Vespasian, Adrian, and other emperors decided lawsuits not only when they were seated on the throne of justice, but also in their rooms at any hour, even during their meals, and even when they were sick in bed. Mithridates, a very powerful king, had learned twenty-two languages in order to be able to hear the supplications of the people who spoke them. Our own Saint Louis was no less concerned about this
163 obligation. In the middle of his recreation, which he usually took in the woods of Vincennes, he would take his place at the foot of an oak tree, and there he would give free audience to anyone who came. With the advice of a few lords who attended him, he would pronounce immediate sentence. I know that a prince cannot be everywhere at once, so it is not necessary that he try to hear quarrels all the time. However, he should at least devote a few days a week to his subjects, as Charlemagne did. He should let them approach him when they have a legitimate complaint. This will prevent many miscarriages of justice and will compel judges, advocates, and prosecutors to walk the straight and narrow when they see that the prince will inform himself about their actions. Similarly Philip the Tall ordered two lords of his court to attend the meetings of Parliament in order to observe and to report to him the activities there and to oppose any censurable statutes. By another ordonnance of Philip the Fair, presiding
164 judges must render an accounting every three years.

Such rigorous measures will not be necessary if one elects magistrates who are old enough, have good judgment, stability, integrity, and good health, and if they have the ability to withstand the temptation of favor, and are not swayed by fear. In a word, they will not hesitate to sign a just petition and cannot be wheedled into signing an unjust one. It is no small matter to be a judge. The lives and property of every man depend on this office. The Athenians accepted in the court of Areopagus only those of noble extraction and exemplary life. Thus, it was the most august and famous consistory ever to exist. It is even said that wicked men who by graft or by dissimulation of their vices had managed to be received into this court, abruptly changed their natures and became good men as though they had been divinely touched by the spirit of the place and of that notable assemblage.

Now, since such perfection does not exist in our country, the prince must be all the more careful to be
aware of the conduct of his judges and to review it with 165
his council, as he does other important matters. Above all, he must enjoin them to expedite lawsuits without wasting their time on unnecessary formalities. Precipitous judgment is unwise, but so is unwarranted delay. It is wrong to defer action on a proceeding when it is apparent where justice lies just because those who do not have a good case wish to prolong the proceeding *ad infinitum* with their little hoaxes. Sometimes the fault lies with the judges who are too slow to re-open a case and are too indulgent toward quibblers who are never at a loss for a trick that will allow them to postpone or confuse a case. The judges should cut short, even punish, such persons, for they give the people cause to murmur against the most sacred order in the

world, since it is so difficult to obtain justice. The resolution of cases is not so involved that it requires so many postponements. If it is a question of fact, then
166 investigation or testimony will clear it up. None of this requires great subtlety. Questions involving a man's rights are for the most part decided by laws, edicts, customs, and precedents. There is not, after all, an unlimited number of complications and negotiations possible. If there is some different circumstance, it is easy to see whether or not it is an important one. Often people make a mountain out of a molehill, and the lawyers with their manner and their routine always find some excuse for holding up a suit.

Besides this, the legal experts, instead of clarifying an issue, often obscure it by their interpretations. This vice is of long standing. Over 1600 years ago Cicero complained that the experts of his day, in order to create the impression of competence in their profession, took a simple hypothesis and divided and subdivided it in order to make it appear difficult. The text of the laws is clear and intelligible to all. If there is some defect, let the judges clear it up with their wisdom and equity.
167 There is no need to have recourse to thousands of interpreters who can never agree among themselves any more than clocks can. Their diverse opinions just cause qualms and distractions. This is what produces and fosters lawsuits and makes them last so long that no one can ever see the end. This is why the Spanish peoples in the Indies were right in begging the king not to send them any lawyers. Uncivilized people, living in a state of nature, are more at ease in these matters than those who deceive with their subtleties.

Since lawsuits are so entrenched in European countries that it is impossible to get rid of them, there is a need to prevent their multiplying and to order that they be settled as promptly as possible. The Roman Senate had a good custom for criminal cases. The senators continued the audience for three consecutive days during which they heard at their leisure the testimony of the parties themselves and their witnesses. They never left the chamber before the sun set. Vespasian had a good method for dealing with civil cases. When he saw that the passage of time had allowed
the dockets to become filled, he chose a group of men 168
and charged them with examining the cases carefully and passing judgment on those that looked as though they could not be settled during the lifetime of the litigants. It is unwise to prolong a suit. This produces an effect similar to that brought on by the use of arms, there is nothing that impoverishes a people more in time of peace, except taxes, of course, which are always the cause of loud complaints.

I would not agree with Nero, however, who resolved to free his subjects from all taxes. A monarch needs some contributions to maintain his status and to make his state secure. But he must use moderation in this matter. He should not be amused by the flatterer's maxim, "There is no worse graft than the people's." This sort of person destroys the mutual friendship that ought to exist between a prince and his subjects. History gives us an infinite number of examples of changes wrought in a state by taxation. Since taxes were first levied to underwrite the cost of war and since our kings
still claim that the taxes will disappear when the cause 169

does, what pretext will they have for continuing them in time of a general peace? The manner in which taxes are levied is the greatest evil. It is not enough to make the poor pay as much as the rich. The most common way is for the rich to pay nothing at all and for the others to bear the entire burden. To correct this inequity, taxes should always be levied on real estate as they are in Provence and Languedoc, or they should be mixed as they were in Rome where everyone paid according to his means and filed a formal declaration of his property. Those who concealed their true wealth were rigorously punished. A revival of this custom was recently attempted, but some were opposed to it for rather frivolous reasons. The Romans found it very effective, and Livy praises it as being the best and healthiest policy that a great monarchy can have. This method of registration can reveal not only how much wealth, but
170 also what resources exist among the people. A record of the age, strength, and condition of all the inhabitants should be kept; it would then be known how many soldiers could be furnished and maintained in time of need.

Seeing that the Turks were making preparations to invade his state, the last Emperor of Constantinople decided, a little late, to take a census of his capital city. He found such a small number of men there who could bear arms that he was forced to keep the results secret and enjoin the men who had prepared the lists not to reveal their contents. Now if, at the very beginning of his reign, he had found out about his people, he would have had enough time to correct the situation. Leaving to one side the other possible uses of the census, we can easily see how important it would be for the matter at hand. Everyone could be taxed in accordance with his ability to pay. Otherwise the poor will be unjustly exploited in the levying of taxes.

There is another abuse implicit in all of this too, that is, the monies pass through so many hands. This is 171
especially true in France, where as it was pointed out to one of our kings, for every *écu* collected not even a *teston* reaches the king's coffers, the rest having been spent for the officers' upkeep. To guard against this, the Turks have very few persons handling the finances. How do they do it? They neither sell estates nor make them hereditary. Conclusion: These two things, excessive taxes and the veniality of office holders, are two of the worst sources of waste in a monarchy. The prince has other, more legitimate means of revenue. And, even if he should have only his personal property and ordinary rights, he would still be able to maintain his court in a resplendent manner without inventing new subsidies. Should the title to his private estate be tied up or transferred to another because of some unfortunate circumstances in the past, he ought to buy it back. It is common knowledge that no one can sell anything for half of what it is worth; certainly the people would gladly contribute to such a good cause in order to be relieved of the burden they are now carrying. This is how a prince should begin the management of his finances, although he can increase them honestly by imposing a tax on the merchandise imported or exported from his country.

A prince has a right to share the profits of those who 172
trade in his domain and in its goods. If the merchandise

being transported should be necessities of life, he need not fear levying a substantial tax on them as well as on the luxuries brought into his kingdom. In this respect he need make no distinction between the merchant who is his subject and the one who is a foreigner, as some princes do today. The conditions laid down for trade ought to apply equally to everyone, particularly in a time of universal peace when it is essential to be on good terms with all. If a prince really wants to make a profit, then he should trade and send his own vessels to sea just as private individuals do. Why should he not follow the example of the merchant rather than of the tyrant or extortioner? It is folly to think that being a merchant is degrading to the nobility. This may be true of peddlers, inn-keepers, and other petty shop clerks,
173 but it is not true of men who send their agents into many provinces to make an honest profit by serving the public. For this reason, many princes today scoff at such scruples, recognizing that there is no more legitimate way of making money than by trade.

I am not speaking here of diving for pearls nor of mining from which many kings have realized a large profit. Nor am I speaking of confiscations or other related business that can greatly augment their treasuries. They also have another means formerly used by the Roman emperors, namely, lending money at five percent interest on good security. This would be very useful to the poor, for they would no longer be fleeced by usurers and would have the use of the prince's money by paying a small rate of interest. Moreover, the prince would realize a good profit if he lent a considerable sum and invested his capital wisely.

However, he must first free his own estates from debt, for there is no possibility of lending when in debt oneself, and still less of storing up an adequate provision
of grains, as must be done to guard against famine or 174
any other public need that might arise.

It was the first duty of the Roman magistrates to maintain storehouses of wheat which they had shipped from many different places, especially from Africa and Egypt. The Africans shipped grain to them for eight months of the year and the Egyptians for four. It wheat was excessively high, the magistrates incurred the hatred of the people who reviled them and even attacked their persons, throwing mud, stones, or manure on them, as happened to the consul Bibulus. They did not even spare the emperors. Witness Claudius, at whom they hurled bits of bread and horrible curses right in the market place. If he had not fled, he would have exposed himself to even greater danger. The good Antonius was stoned in a similar riot. Such a thing could be prevented if, as Joseph did, one were to provide a wheat supply sufficient for several years. It would be carefully guarded and replenished in public granaries established in every city. That is what used to be done, and the
custom is still continued in some well-managed cities. 175

It is not, however, expedient to supply the people with free grain as they used to do in ancient Rome. Such a practice would cause the people to become lazy and would exhaust the public treasury. Still less should we follow the example of Nicephorus Phocas who filled his granaries with wheat and resold it at leisure when the price was high. What is needed is a sufficient supply to sell at a just price in a time of crop failure and famine.

Here, the prince will show his foresight and concern for his subjects who complain when they do not see wheat for sale in the market. They blame their sovereign for a bad year as though he were responsible for the temperature of the air and the favor of the heavens. In fact, kings in the Indies obligated themselves by a solemn oath at the time of their coronation to see to it that the sun continued in its proper course and that the earth brought forth an abundant harvest. So the people must be satisfied in this respect, because, as the satirical poet said, above all else they require bread and circuses.

176 This is an appropriate introduction to our sixth point, the legitimate pastimes in which it is good to encourage men to participate in order to deter them from evil thoughts. Since everyone is naturally inclined to pleasure, it is prudent for the prince to give or permit his people some honest and legitimate diversions. Athletic events, the theater, and other recreational exercises are examples of pastimes which do not waste one's patrimony and which make the body healthy and the mind content. It was the aim of the wrestling matches, the races, and the poetry and music contests in ancient times not only to strengthen the body and encourage the best efforts of the participants, but also to entertain the audience. Tragedies and comedies had the same goal. The Athenians used the municipal treasury and chose a special magistrate to pay the expenses of the players. The Romans imitated and even surpassed them, for, besides the pleasure derived from the theater, they had the spectacles of the Circus
177 Maximus, the Colesseum, the naumachias, which the magistrates vied with one another to make more and

more magnificient.

Some condemn comedies as being detrimental to morals because of their lasciviousness. At Marseille, they abhorred and expressly forbade them. Their opinion is not valid, however, for nothing should ever be condemned merely because it has been abused. If, among so many speeches, the comedians should let one risqué passage slip out, their art as a whole should not be any less esteemed, since it is only an image of life, a representation of what is done and not a recommendation of what ought to be done. Is it not ridiculous to blame comedy while furnishing it with material, to take pleasure in vicious actions, and to loathe the words that describe them? Men do not leave the theater with corrupted morals. They were corrupt before entering. Let them conduct their reforms in their own homes, and farces and comedies will die out. Let them set a good example for their families, and they need no longer fear the corruption of youth. But as long
as wrongdoing and evil still exist, there will be a need to 178
bring them to light so that the people will avoid them or ridicule them.

Aristotle approved of such pastimes, and even the Church Fathers recommend them, with certain modifications, as a very necessary thing. Since men are made up of both soul and body, and since these two substances are limited, they cannot stand to work all of the time. Therefore, they must be permitted some relaxation and pleasure. The theater provides the best means of obtaining this end, for it delights both the eye and the ear. Philosophers have called these pleasures "human" to distinguish them from brute pleasures, namely those of taste and touch. In short, such pastimes should not be forbidden for even the wise Socrates went to hear the buffoon, Aristophanes, and the serious-minded Cato wanted to see the festivals at the Floralia.

Nevertheless, to give pleasure to which no scandal is
179 attached, music seems to me to be the most suitable of all, given that everyone loves it, except a few unfeeling souls or those whose sense of values is distorted. Certainly we are naturally disposed to harmony and listen to its sweet tones with more attentiveness and delight than we do anything else. Its marvelous effects have forced the two shrewdest philosophers to say that to regulate morals, one must regulate music, and that the welfare of a state is dependent on it. I shall not stop to analyze this comment, but it is undeniable that there is nothing better able to make men more calm and more peaceable. The people of Arcadia are a case in point. They became ferocious and cruel when they abandoned music which, according to the custom of that country, everyone had to practice until the age of thirty. What must the Emperor Soliman have thought when Francis I sent him singers with lutes, violas, and selected music as a present? For a while he took the time to listen to
180 them, but when he saw that his court was enjoying them, he sent them away and had their instruments and books burned. This was a barbaric act based on the false assumption that music makes men effeminate. As if Achilles had lost his nobility by playing on his lyre, or the Spartans were less valiant because they went into battle accompanied by the music of flutes!

Music in no way blunts the edge of courage. Instead,

it awakens a mysterious response in us and incites us to
virtue by touching the soul with divine pleasure and by
uprooting little by little all inhumanity and evil. The
uncultured call this weakness and cowardice; but they
are mistaken, for vices have nothing in common with
gentleness and mildness, virtues suitable for any man. If
music should change morals in any way, and even the
most beneficial things sometimes have a bad effect
through improper use, then it would be the duty of the
censors to correct this abuse as they would any other.
Such a magistrate is necessary to perfect our policies. He
has the responsibility of taking the census and of 181
reforming morals. As for the census, we have already
demonstrated its utility. Reform, however, is of even
greater importance. Nothing good can be expected of a
kingdom where morals are not regulated. Judges are of
no help in establishing order, for they only punish
crimes and contrive to ignore many vices that
imperceptibly undermine the state. They do not censure
children who disobey their fathers. They allow
libertines, procurers, perjurers, gamblers, owners of
gambling houses, drunkards, and quarrelsome and idle
persons to remain free. Yet, it is with such people that
sedition and the ruin of republics originate. I realize that
they should not be punished as severly as thieves and
murderers, and, moreover, that the censors' power does
not extend to execution and imprisonment. The Roman
censors could only make public the names of those
leading dissolute lives and humiliate each one according
to his condition. Thus, if the delinquent was a Senator, 182
he was forbidden to enter the council; a knight lost his
title; a simple citizen, his civic rights.

This ignominy had more effect than all the laws and ordonnances of the judges. And while it brought more shame than actual harm, there was no man so bold that he did not fear the judgment of the censor. It is true that no one could hold this office who did not have authority by virtue of his age and integrity. The fear of dishonor serves as a check to halt the wickedest of men. While they may pretend not to care, it is nonetheless true that many do not want to be known for what they are, nor to be laughed at by the people, which is what would happen to them after they had been struck from the rolls and treated ignominiously by the censors. Then you would see these good-for-nothings going about with their heads down, not daring to appear in company. People would point them out so as to be able to flee them like the plague. They would serve as an example to
183 teach others to live honestly.

Some may say that such severity would not be acceptable today, and that modern man cannot be governed as the ancients were. I would answer that this idea is false and contrary to experience, reason, and the authority of the wise man who said, "There is nothing new under the sun." Actions and events occur in new circumstances, but the types have always been the same. The same measures that upheld monarchies of long ago can preserve them today; they can also be destroyed by the same means as they used to be. To see disorder and to be unwilling to correct it, to refuse to try, merely because what has been proposed is not new, is a cowardly and malicious way to act. Such sallies are commonly used by persons who don't know what to say or who don't think anything is valid unless it is their own

idea. Thus, they are not the ones whose advice we should seek on the question of reestablishing the censorship. When it is a question of confiscating bad merchandise, you do not ask the advice of the one who 184
is selling it. When lawmakers set up punishments they did not take into consideration the feelings of the guilty, nor did they consult those who had committed the crimes. Therefore, let kings reinstate the censorship, paying no attention to those who have a stake in its continued absence. Let them not deliberate on whether or not they should reform morals, since it is a necessary thing. It held the Roman empire together for a long time and is used by some republics today.

Now to get this reform off to a good start, we must begin by instructing the young. A great deal of care used to be given to this task, but today it is almost ignored, since the magistrates leave it to the parents, and the parents have slackened the reins that they used to have on their children. This neglect is all the more dangerous in our age when parental authority has been abolished. When fathers had sovereign authority over their children, they punished them as they saw fit, and even executed them without stating why, for justice presupposed that a man would not be so unnatural as to beat or kill his son without good reason. Now that the 185
fear of this parental authority has been removed, and the children enjoy such license that they lay down the law to their fathers and sometimes even injure them by open attack or by words, the republic must take over this responsibility in order to avoid the misfortune that might result from such a state of affairs. Magistrates should be specifically instructed to be particularly

careful of these young trees so that they may bring forth good fruit. The Lacedemonians, who understood this very well, did not permit fathers to bring up their children in any way that suited them, but rather put the children into groups as soon as they were seven years old. An especially selected magistrate was put in charge of these groups and had them eat and drink together publicly and accustomed them to the same exercises. Where they failed was in limiting these exercises almost entirely to wrestling, for besides the fact that wrestling is too violent and can easily injure the delicate bodies of
186 children, they learn to become haughty, quarrelsome, and barbaric, qualities not suitable for public instruction. Aristotle thought it more beneficial to train them in the liberal arts.

To make myself perfectly clear, I should advise that up to the age of fourteen they should be taught to read, write, and count. In addition, they should acquire some knowledge of the laws and ancient customs of their country, as the Roman children used to learn the laws of the Twelve Tables by heart. In order to make the process of learning their laws easier and more pleasant for the children, the Cretans set them to music. Besides that, they familiarized them with songs in honor of the gods and famous men. These were all lessons in honor. Such teaching deserves to be brought back. I should also be in favor of children's learning the foreign languages most popular in their culture, as Greek and Latin have been among Christians and Arabic among Moham-
187 medans. This branch of knowledge would not be without its utility, since it would enlighten their minds and help them, when they were older, should they wish

to go into the study of theology, medicine, law, and philosophy. If not, they could always boast that they had not wasted their childhood, as so many do who are accustomed from the cradle to fritter away their time and romp about, with the result that after a time they know nothing but inanities. Is it not better to acquaint children with worthwhile disciplines, until such time as they are stronger? Then it will be proper to have them exercise their minds and their bodies alternately so that they will be able not only to speak effectively and make sound judgments, but also to defend themselves courageously in case of necessity. To this end, from fourteen to eighteen, they will learn how to manage a horse, swim, jump, and fire arms while continuing with the first kind of exercise I have specified above. Having reached eighteen, they would return to their fathers who would be very pleased. As the Gauls did not want to see their children until they could bear arms, so
everyone would rejoice to see his son able to function in 188
either war or peace. He would have him adopt a vocation suitable to his station in life, and instead of the difficult children we have today, a father would find his son amenable to his commands and to reason; this would be the result of the good education he had received.

Moreover, the prince would have a breeding ground for counsellors and men-at-arms who could assist him in case of need. He would know who could be of use to him in whatever capacity, and, without having recourse to foreigners, would easily find among his own subjects, an unlimited number of good officers, soldiers, and artisans. There is certainly nothing of greater

importance than the education of youth. It is the foundation of the state and the basis for the tranquility we are seeking. The censors ought, therefore, to keep an eye on it, and, so that no one will drift into idleness, they will require everyone to choose an occupation as soon as he has left the public academy. I cannot approve of the custom of the Egyptians and the Spartans who required every child to follow the occupation of his
189 father, with the result that the son of a cook was a cook, and the son of a court crier could not aspire to any more honorable station. To do this is to close the door to virtue and industry.

It is better to give the young a free choice so that they will adopt the profession to which their natures and abilities incline them, subject to the pleasure of the prince, however, by whom they must be authorized in order to follow a given calling. If everyone wanted to choose the same one, the public would be seriously affected. This is why it is necessary to have some controls, so that in every city there will be enough men in all of the trades and so that some do not multiply excessively and thereby weaken the republic. It is not right for all subjects to be soldiers. The unfortunate results that might arise from this situation were accurately foreseen by Francis I, and he therefore demoted all the legionnaires. Neither is it expedient to have so many judges, priests, monks, prosecuting attorneys, advocates, practitioners, and sergeants, too
190 many of whom weaken a kingdom. All such persons must be reduced to a certain number of proportion to the size of their city or province.

The censors can easily see to this matter, because

they are charged with keeping account of the number of people and of recording the name and occupation of each. As for gentlemen, their number cannot be limited, since this depends on the fortunes of the noble families. It will suffice to make them adhere to their obligations through fear of the disgrace a discreditable action might entail. They, like everyone else, should be subject to the censure in all questions concerning the regulation of morals. As regards workers, artisans, laborers, and in general all merchants who trade on land or sea, the greatness and the wealth of states depend entirely on them. Thus, an increase in their number is no cause for alarm. Care need only be taken to assure that they do not begin to compete with one another and that each remain in the province of his own trade in order to avoid confusion and strife. It is by these means that peace will be maintained within each individual 191
monarchy.

There are other, more universal ways based on common agreement among monarchs. The first and most important of these is that they be content with the boundaries prescribed for their domains by the general assembly of which we have spoken. Once this point has been agreed upon, methods must be sought by which the individuals of different nations may meet and trade with one another safely. It should also be clearly understood that should any lawsuit or dispute arise among them, the magistrates of the place in question may settle it without showing favor or partiality to anyone. Since universal peace is at issue, justice must be accorded foreigners; the natives of the country to which they come either for business or pleasure must not be

allowed to harm them in any way. The Romans had a praetor whose duty it was to judge foreigners' cases. It
192 would be wise to have one in every city and village where people often rob and injure foreigners without fear or reprisal because of the collusion of the magistrates who give outsiders no satisfaction at all. However, injuries done individuals sometimes cause wars between countries. The Swiss banded together against the Duke of Burgundy to avenge a wrong done one of their townsmen from whom a cartload of sheepskins had been stolen.

Now once universal peace has been established, there will almost certainly be a few troublemakers who will try to disturb it by all manner of tricks. They will try to accomplish their design by heaping a thousand indignities on foreign merchants and by attacking their persons or their goods in order to estrange them and sever communications, which is the only bond of friendship and alliance. Therefore it will be necessary, for fear that someone be forced to indulge in reprisals, which can only disrupt the peace, for each prince to protect foreigners from his own subjects in case they should molest them. I say "from his own subjects," for
193 it is not just to protect a man from the sovereign against whom he has revolted. Francis I was ill-advised in this respect when he gave asylum to Robert de la Marche to protect him from Charles V, and a few years later, to correct this fault of too generous a heart, he refused the very advantageous offers of the people of Ghent who implored his aid against the same prince. Yet he would have been more justified in taking the side of these people inasmuch as they were naturally his subjects,

having formerly been French citizens. Louis XI committed the same error when he made himself the protector of Liège.

This is why in peace treaties one ordinarily finds a clause to the effect that the allied princes will not grant asylum to one another's subjects if the persons who seek it do not have their sovereign's consent. This custom was followed by the allies of Rome. They stipulated expressly that their citizens should not be granted Roman citizenship without their permission. Our chroniclers tell us that according to the agreement made
between Gontran and Childebert, two French kings, 194
neither of them was to sollicit or attract his companion's subjects. A similar article is found in the treaties of alliance between the Kings of France and the Swiss. Since the greatness of princes is primarily dependent upon the number of their vassals and subjects, they must not permit them to disband and change domicile at pleasure. Those who have offended their sovereign by some evil act or disservice should be even less entitled to this liberty. After all, we are not looking for a hollow peace nor for one lasting only three days, but for one that will be voluntary, equal, and permanent, a peace that will grant everyone what belongs to him: full privileges to every citizen, hospitality to the stranger, and freedom to travel and trade to everyone without exception.

The Lacedemonians were wrong to expel foreigners from their city. The Lucanians' custom was much more honest. They made anyone who turned a traveler away
from his door in the evening pay a fine. The Athenians, 195
Cretans, Romans, and all noble peoples have been

hospitable, recognizing that man is a social animal who has an obligation to help his neighbors as far as his means permit and that he ought likewise to receive the same courtesy from them.

Now, as commerce and communication among peoples is maintained by money, which circulates among countries, it is necessary to standardize prices, weights and their relative value and to resolve to make no innovations in this area on any pretext whatsoever. If there is any doubt about whether a certain coin is legal tender or about its exact value, then contracts will be uncertain, and no one will ever be sure of what he has. The prince must not alter the standard of a given piece of money for a whim, otherwise he will endanger others and will find no one willing to trade with him. Now in this matter there are two interrelated abuses, that is, the reduction of the amount of precious metals in coins and the fluctuation in their value. The trouble all stems from the admixture of these three metals: gold, silver and copper. Since they were mixed for the works goldsmiths
196 produced and for statuary, men have done the same with money. Some have been more conscientious about this than others and have altered and adulterated gold and silver less, retaining more gold and silver in their alloys than their neighbors. This should not be very surprising to anyone, inasmuch as the degree of fineness varies from place to place within a country.

Everyone knows that the *sous* now current in France are not nearly so pure as those at the time of St. Louis, and that those dating from that time do not meet the standard as well as the quarter of an *écu* or the twenty-*sou* pieces. This is what causes a rise in the price of hard money. The hard pieces are cleverly retired by foreign and native merchants who melt them down and make other coins with less metal in them. They then pass them off in payment to the people, who accept this defective money as though it were genuine, not knowing how to distinguish between the two. Then they are amazed to see their sub-standard money discredited and the remaining pieces of hard money so inflated in price because of their scarcity. The result is that a person who thought he had a quarter of an *écu* in his purse doesn't have a twentieth of one.

This brings more hardship to the French than to
other nations. If, instead of raising, they lowered the 197
price of gold and silver, foreigners who have large amounts of these metals on hand would be forced to bring them into this kingdom to buy at a high price the goods they cannot do without, such as wheat, wine, salt, and other food stuffs. These items cost them almost nothing because we place too high a value on their gold. Besides that, to make an even greater profit, they bring us pearls, silks, perfumes, and other trifles, which they give us in exchange for necessities, or which they sell for their value in gold. In time of peace, we have seen the gold mark increase in value by 38 pounds over a period of twelve years. If we count from the year 1577 to 1602, it has increased by 56 pounds 6½ *sous*. I know that the necessities of business may justify this rise, as in the reign of Charles VII. In the year 1422, the
gold mark was valued at 2,847 pounds, the *écu* was 198
worth up to 40 pounds, and the silver mark 360 pounds. But the turmoil of that time caused this inflation, and when order was re-established, these metals were

restored to their usual value, for everyone realized that their higher cost was having an adverse effect on both public and private capital. For someone who had lent 100 *écus* in gold in August of the year 1602, if he were patient until the year 1614, would receive, because of inflation, only 80 *écus* if he insisted on being paid in gold. It is true that it is not to his advantage to accept payment in specie as long as inflation continues and is the same everywhere. Nor is it to his advantage to do this if the value of merchandise does not rise on this account, as is usually the case.

I know that a certain person maintained, in a book he had published on this subject, that there is a great deal to be lost on one piece of gold and silver, even if it is disposed of at the same price for which it was received. He proves this in the following way: *A burgher in the*
199 *time of King John who had 36 pounds income from rent or investments, received, to pay this revenue, 36 gold francs valued at that time at the rate of 20 sous each or the equivalent in silver coin. For these 36 gold francs he could buy 9 hogsheads of wine at 4 pounds each in the money of that time or 4 gold francs which are now worth 12 pounds each. If the burgher is now paid the said revenue, i.e. 36 pounds, in the said gold francs he can today buy only 3 hogsheads of wine, since each hogshead now costs 12 pounds, whereas he formerly could have bought 9 hogsheads. Thus, he loses 6 hogsheads of wine on his 12 gold francs, even though he invested them at the same rate as he got them, i.e. 60 sous.*

At the time of St. Louis the gentleman or anyone of whatever rank who had 16 pounds of rent or revenue

received in payment of this sum 5 pure silver marks or the equivalent in gold coin, for the pure silver mark at that time was worth only 64 of the coins called "sous" 200
or "gros tournois."[1] *To pay him this revenue today, one would give him only one pure silver mark, which is only one-fifth of the silver contained in the original 16 pounds. For 16 pounds at that time he could buy 16 ells of cloth at 2 sous an ell that was as good or better than what now costs 10 sous minted at Tours. At the present time for 16 pounds one can buy only 3 ells, one-fifth of the cloth, at 100 sous an ell instead of the 16 possible at the earlier period. This represents a loss of 12 ells, or four-fifths of the cloth on a 16 pound purchase, even though each pound were placed at the same price for which it was received, namely 20 sous. If we figure by the sou or by the douzain, we shall find that the result is the same. For 10 sous, formerly received by the gentleman from his rents or lands, containing as much pure silver as the 50 sous pieces of today, he could buy 5 capons at the rate of 2 sous apiece. Now for 10 sous he can buy only 1 capon, a loss of 4 capons on a 10 sous purchase, even though he had placed the said sous at 12 deniers each, which is the same price at which he received them.*

This is the said gentleman's demonstration of his theory to which he adds another paradox, namely that nothing has become more expensive in France in the last 201
300 years. *One may not complain,* he says, *that a thing has become more expensive in the last 300 years, unless, in order to buy it, it is necessary to put out more gold or silver than in the past. Now the fact is that to buy something today one does not pay out more gold or*

silver than before. For in the time of Philip of Valois, who began his reign in the year 1328, an ell of velvet cost 4 écus as good, nay better in weight and value than our écus presently in circulation. Each écu was worth only 20 sous in silver coin, whereas now the écu is worth 50 sous and the ell of velvet costs 10 pounds. Nevertheless, to pay these 10 pounds, one needs the said sum of 4 écus, worth 50 sous each, as the law dictates, or the equivalent in silver coin. Therefore the ell of velvet is no more expensive now, than it was then. That is his reasoning, but it is sophistic, and only appears to be true, because its major premise, which he presupposes to be incontestable, and which even Bodin grants him without thinking, is, in fact, false. This is because things are not bought only with gold and silver,
202 but with copper, which makes a third species of coin, of less value. Copper, although the least valuable, nevertheless regulates the price of all the others, as in Rome an *asse* of brass was the basis for determining the value of the *sesterce*, the *denier*, and other larger coins, because the *sesterce* was worth 2½ *asses*, and a silver *denarius* was worth 10. The value of this last coin was raised and set at 16 *asses*. In questions of weight, measure, and coin, the smallest is the measure of the largest.

This being so, I contend that the worth of coins lies only in the value placed on them, so that if the latter increases, their worth is similarly increased. Consequently the standard *écu*, when it is worth only 20 *sous*, that is 230 *deniers*, is not as valuable as when it is worth 60 *sous* or 720 *deniers*, because its value must be measured in the small coins. Furthermore, gold and silver are only

as valuable as the prince and the people choose to make
them. Thus, in Lacedemonia, when iron money was in 203
use, gold and silver were superfluous. Today in Ethiopia, where salt is money, gold is useless for commerce. Also, the brass of which we are speaking was more precious than gold among certain Oriental peoples according to Joseph's report.

It is therefore erroneous to conclude that velvet is not more expensive than it used to be merely because one pays only 4 gold *écus* just as one used to do. For the *écus* paid out now, even though they be the same kind as in the past, are worth more and cost more than they did, since they are equivalent to more, smaller coins.

If the pure silver *sous* that St. Louis had forged were still extant, they would be worth three or four times more than they were in the beginning, because at that time they were valued at only 12 *deniers.* Today, however, from one of those *sous* three or four could be minted, each worth 12 *deniers.* When the Romans lowered the weight of the *asse,* while keeping its
ordinary valuation, and made six out of one, those who 204
had the old *asses,* weighing a pound, were five times richer than before. If they owed four *asses,* they could not, without hurting themselves, repay them to their creditors in the same coin, nor could the creditors accept them without being guilty of usury because of the new valuation the people had given this money. This valuation is the true and essential worth of a coin. This being the case, we can infer the absurdity of the major premise of the same author when he says that anyone having 36 good francs of revenue would not get them today. For even though he would not receive them in

specie, he would receive the same value, which is the equivalent. If, for 12 *écus*, he cannot, as formerly, buy 9 hogsheads of wine, that does not result from the increase in the price of gold, since it does not follow necessarily that merchandise becomes more expensive because of the increased value of coins.

There are many other causes of increased prices,
205 namely, luxury, the abundance of gold and silver, and
monopolies. Moreover, the author we have quoted becomes entangled in his concepts, for on the one hand he denies the increase of prices, and on the other he gives examples of that very thing. This is an obvious contradiction, which is what I wanted to show in passing in order to compensate for Bodin's mistake, since he did not give the result of his reasonings but contented himself with setting forth his line of reasoning without answering the question directly. I admit, however, that the excessive rise in the value of coins is prejudicial for the reasons set forth above, and that it is necessary for princes, by common consent, to standardize these values so that everyone can do business everywhere without loss.

Many solutions to this dilemma have been suggested and merit being put into practice. First, a proposal has been made that all countries agree on one price for a gold mark and make twelve pounds of silver equal to one pound of gold. This proportion used to be accepted and is still kept, more or less, in many parts of the world. The King of the Indies in the time of Augustus, was amazed to see that his subjects agreed with the
206 Romans on this policy. Secondly, many are of the
opinion that copper alloys should be forbidden, as some

kings have already done, because they permit falsifying or debasing the coins. Now, these coins are never the same, with the result that those who understand parity amass as many good coins as they can so that they can melt them down and make new ones with less metal, thereby making a profit. This results in an incredible loss to the people. They would be unable to do this if coins were pure gold and silver, for when a common metal is substituted for another, the color, weight, volume, ring, and other properties make the deception easily detectable, whereas it is very difficult to recognize the quality and value of such diverse and unequal alloys as we now use. This is another reason why it is expedient to forbid, on pain of death, the mixing of metals to everyone in general and to minters, jewellers, and goldsmiths in particular.

Such a regulation would require that all of their work be done in pure metals, and it would also uncover any frauds that might be perpetrated. Still, since the
complete refining of gold and silver is impossible 207
without loss and great expense, the time-honored regulations of this kingdom should be followed. They require that gold used by the goldsmith or the coiner be 23 carats and that silver be refined to 11 *deniers* 12 grains. If this procedure is adopted, moreover, the ratio between gold and silver will be maintained, given that the mixtion in each will always be the same; that is, there will be only 1/24 of another metal in all gold or silver works. The people will then be able to exchange gold for silver, without loss, at the rate of 12 pounds of silver for one pound of gold according to the policy we have just mentioned. This will be possible because the

two metals will be equally refined.

To allow these two metals to be mixed with baser ones, as we do today, is to give free rein to counterfeiters to falsify coins. It is no less dangerous to allow differing laws on these matters in the different provinces, since the most stable coins in circulation in any country are carefully withdrawn by thrifty, enterprising men who convert them into less valuable coins circulating in another country. Frequently,
208 goldsmiths and refiners use them for their work, since they will then have full benefit of the purity of the gold and silver; coins made of alloy are left for the people. These two drawbacks are rather well-known, especially the first, since Castillian *reales*, because of their value, have been converted by a number of sovereigns into the money of their country, and they have thereby realized a handsome profit. The Swiss did the same thing with French *testons* from which they forged their own *testons*, which were equal to ours neither in quality nor in weight.

Princes are not content with merely lowering the quality of their coins; they also diminish their weight without reducing their valuation at all. The *sou* piece, which used to weigh four *deniers*, was reduced, during the reign of Francis I, to two *deniers* sixteen grains and was further debased under Charles IX. Other sovereigns have not been any more conscientious. Witness the Spanish coins which, under Charles V, were lightened by three grains. Following his example, all the Italian lords
209 forged coins weighing only two *deniers* sixteen grains and refined to only 22 carats at most. We suspect that the further we go, the more the necessities of war,

luxury, and prodigality will force princes to devalue their coins, unless they make an agreement among themselves to forge coins only of a given quality and weight. As far as quality is concerned, it is easy to standardize it by following the rule stated above.

Weight is a more difficult problem because of the great diversity of standards. Things have reached the point where it is difficult to find two monarchies that use the same system. Even within one kingdom, France, for example, a distinct difference is found between one city and another in the weights used. This is especially true of the gold and silver mark, the standard weight for money or the goldsmith's art. Although this mark is everywhere said to weigh eight ounces, it is nevertheless very different because ounces are heavier in some places than in others: seven ounces in Geneva is equivalent to almost eight in Paris. On the other hand, it takes scarcely more than five Parisian ounces to weigh as 210
much as the mark at Piedmont, Milan, and Genoa. This hampers trade and gives unscrupulous merchants an opportunity to cheat foreigners by giving them a false idea of a weight with which they are unfamiliar. Whatever foresight kings may have, they will never be able to prevent swindlers from buying at a high weight and selling at a low one. This will continue as long as there are such differences within their own state or in their neighbors', or in those with which they trade.

This is why it is necessary for all of them to agree on a common regulation by which not only gold and silver, but also merchandise, shall be sold at equal weights in all countries. This will not be difficult to do; nature's works, namely grains, will serve as a guide for our

weights and measures. As for measures, the league has traditionally been equal to two miles, the mile to eight furlongs, the furlong to 125 paces, the pace to five feet,
211 the foot to four hands, the hand to four fingers, and a finger to four grains. Concerning weights, we come back again to the grain as a measure for all the others. The mark contains eight ounces; the ounce is equal to eight drams or *gros* and is also the equivalent of 24 *deniers*, each being worth 3 *deniers*. The *denier* weighs 24 grains. This rule is still valid today in several kingdoms and was used in ancient Greece, because it is indeed very suitable for trade purposes. Thus, the ounce weighs 576 grains, the mark 4,608, and the merchant's pound weighs once again more. No doubt if this standard were accepted by all nations, trade would be a great deal easier.

Yet, there is one thing that seems to prevent or diminish its utility, namely the difference in weight among grains. Some kinds weigh more in one place than in another, and therefore they cannot be used to standardize the marks and ounces of different countries,
212 since their measure is varying and unequal. This problem can be resolved if all the sovereigns agree to base all their weights on the grains of a given country, which they can choose by common consent so that, the quality and the weight of the grain being stable, the other weights based on it will also be fixed and cannot be questioned. Now, if each sovereign wants to have his own weights, either to maintain his standing or to eliminate the difficulties involved in making changes, then it will be necessary to evaluate the gold and silver mark by its weight. For, when we have fixed the quality, namely, 23 carats for gold and 11 *deniers* 12

grains for silver, as we have said, and in addition we have accepted the ratio of 1 to 12 between these two metals, according to the ancient custom, the only problems left to consider are their quantity, the price, and the proportion of the metals, so that the mark which weighs 4,608 grains more than another will also have a proportionately higher value. But since its excess weight cannot be settled, except by a common measure, it is 213
more reasonable to practice the regulation mentioned above.

A foreigner can always be made to believe either that his weight is no better than that of the country in which he is trading, even though it may be an ounce or more heavier, or that, if he protests, he will find that there are many witnesses to testify against him. Thus he has only two choices: to let himself be cheated or to return home without having accomplished anything. This sort of thing can easily break off trade, for commerce between nations can flourish only where there is agreement on weights and measures. Even the measures are not so necessary, for some nations, like the Chinese, do not even use them. They are accustomed to weighing everything, even cloth, for they think that it is easier and more common to be deceived where measures are concerned. There can be no doubt that this is true provided there be only one standard of weight, or if there are many, at least the difference should be published and their proportion recognized so as to avoid the cheating that is otherwise inevitable. The regulation ought to apply specifically to the weight of gold and silver where fraud is very likely since it is very lucrative. 214

I therefore contend, to return to our original

proposition, that one needs to standardize not only the quality but also the weight of coins, and in this regard to limit the number of coins manufactured out of one mark of gold or silver, of the same weight, name, and value. Eight, sixteen, thirty-two, or sixty-four of these equal coins can be made out of one mark. More can be made, if necessary, by increasing their number in arithmetical ratio, while still being careful that their small size not make them too fragile. Therefore, the largest coins, of which eight will make a mark, will weigh an ounce each; those that come sixteen to a mark will weigh half an ounce; those having thirty-two to a mark will weigh two drams, and those having sixty-four to a mark will be one dram each. Then, changing from gold to silver, not only in bulk and unworked metal, but also in coin, will be very easy, because, for one piece of gold, people will exchange twelve silver ones of the same weight. This rule will hold good not only among compatriots, but among foreigners as well, since the basis for exchange will be the same everywhere.
215 Therefore there will be no reason to raise it in one country any more than in another.

The only exception would be if princes wished to disrupt this order by exercising their traditional right of seigniorage to levy a tax on coins minted in their lands. This they should do only with the greatest care, and they should think not so much of their own individual profit as of the general good, their reputation, and the example of other sovereigns with whom they should come to an agreement concerning the regulation of such rights. After that, in order to eliminate counterfeiting and coin clipping, it will be expedient to make the coins

in a mould just as ancient medallions were made. The moulds would make all the pieces of the same name and value, equal in width, thickness, weight, and circumference. The counterfeiter could not so easily imitate such coins without being discovered, since the copper substituted for the gold and silver, being much lighter, is greater in volume, for the same weight, than
these two metals. A false piece would then be easy to 216
recognize by comparing it with the standard coin.

Today there are mints that can fulfill this need. The first of these was erected in Paris as early as 1553. Although many do not approve of their use, the fact is that they have more advantages than disadvantages. There has also been very little counterfeiting or clipping of minted coins. Counterfeiters fear that they will be found out by the means we have just described, namely, by comparing the weight and dimensions of a false coin with a legitimate one. Coins of the same denomination and quality will always be identical when made in a mint where the stamping, cutting, and pressing will be the same. This cannot be done with a hammer since it cannot be brought down with a constant force or manipulated accurately enough so as always to give exact measurements. This inequality gives counterfeiters and clippers an opening. They fear nothing more than to see all coins made uniform in terms of their shape,
weight, and volume, because that would deprive them of 217
all means of disguising their frauds.

To impede them even more, we need to renew Charlemagne's edict by which he forbade the forging of coins anywhere but in his palace. Although he possessed a far-flung empire, still he designated only one place for such work. Thus, in a monarchy, one or two cities at most should be chosen to house the mint, so that unscrupulous men will then have less opportunity to be dishonest. The most effective way is still to abolish the use of copper alloys, which are always unequal and uncertain and therefore are not suitable for maintaining the proportion between gold and silver nor for the exchange of these metals. This was recognized in France when they debased the *douzain* of which sixty made an *écu*,[2] [even though] I know that their true worth was less than fifty-three *sous*. For this same reason, I should advise doing away with copper money, because *doubles* and *deniers* were once minted that did not equal the value of the *écu*, although they were commonly valued at nine pounds fifteen *sous*.

218 This is an incredible loss for a lower-class person as well as for church-wardens, beggars, and hospitals; they never receive anything but these small coins. It would therefore be better, in order to make this policy work, to reduce the number of coins to two, as has been done in some kingdoms. From one silver mark could be made as many little coins as can readily be made. They would take the place of copper *doubles* and *deniers* and be used for alms and the purchase of inexpensive goods. It would not be necessary to mint 8,000 coins to the mark as was done in Lorraine. Two thousand would be sufficient, and each coin would be more solid and would last longer.

Now, if you do not want to abolish copper money, and indeed it is difficult to get along without it, at least let it be pure copper, not combined with any other metal, and let its value be fixed, and not variable. This is

what happened in Rome where the silver *denarius*, according to many, weighed as much as the dram or 219
gros of today and was valued at ten *asses*, that is, ten pounds of brass since the pound then was twelve ounces. Thus, a pound of silver was worth 960 pounds of brass. After some time, there was such a reduction in the weight of the *asse* that twenty-four were made out of one, so that they weighed only half an ounce each but had the same valuation as when they weighed a pound. The smallest coin must have a fixed value, because all the others depend on it. Therefore, it is imperative either that the use of copper for money be forbidden entirely, or else that a price be fixed once and for all, as with gold and silver, so that everyone may be sure of what it is worth.

Now, as for copper alloy, I know that to do away with it entirely is to do a great disservice to the common people who will suffer great losses if coins are limited to the standard discussed above. They will have the advantage, however, of being sure in the future that the coins they get are good and will have no cause to fear an 220
increase or a decrease of their value, as happens only too often. The possible resulting loss incurred by having this policy put into effect will never be so great as the usefulness of a general peace. Add to this the fact that the monarch can compensate his people and prevent any discontent caused by such an innovation by lowering the taxes and by making free distributions of wheat or other foodstuffs to the most needy. The monarch should do this so that these people will bear the debasing of their copper patiently, for they and their children will finally reap the benefits. In short, one

should not fear undertaking something necessary and easy to carry out provided that universal peace reigns.

To get this movement underway, one powerful prince must exhort all the others to follow the above-mentioned regulation so that, routes being open and commerce being made possible due to the general peace, people can trade everywhere without fear of loss. No one is better suited for this role than the Pope. It is
221 his duty to effect a general agreement among Christian princes. As for the Mohammedans, who make up a considerable part of the world, the King of France, because of the status and reputation he enjoys among them, will be able most easily to make them consent to peace. The Emperor, and the kings of Spain, Poland, Persia, and Ethiopia would perhaps hesitate to send their ambassadors to the Sultan on this errand thinking that others would be of the opinion that it was fear of his power that was forcing them to seek peace. This consideration would not apply in the case of our king, since he has no occasion to fear the Emperor of the Turks and can honorably undertake this affair, especially given the ancient alliance between the kingdoms of France and Turkey.

However this may be, it is most fitting that the Christians be the first to speak of peace, even if their only aim were to be permitted to visit the Holy Sepulchre. Once they were at peace with the Turks,
222 they could easily get the other monarchs to agree, since these rulers would not be strong enough to resist two such powerful parties. We read that the hermit Simon Camertin brought about a reconciliation between Francesco Sforza and the Venetians. In the last eighty

years the two most powerful Christian princes have
twice been reconciled through the good offices of a
simple monk. All the more reason why we can look
forward to a lasting peace if the sovereigns themselves
take a hand. May God, Who guides the hearts of kings,
grant that they be well-disposed toward so holy an
undertaking, so as to put an end to so many evils and to
usher in that golden age which the ancient theologians
promised will come after 6,000 years have lapsed. They
say that then the world will live happily and at peace.
Now it happens that this period will soon be over, but
even if it were not, the princes need only desire it to be
able to give their people such happiness ahead of time.

What do we hope to accomplish with those arms?
Shall we always live as beasts do? It would be an
improvement if we used as much restraint as they, for
they never fight in large groups and do not even fight 223
with one another unless they are compelled by hunger
or some other necessity. Men stir up trouble with very
little provocation. Sometimes they blithely launch
campaigns, not to engage in single combat, but ten
thousand against ten thousand just to amuse them-
selves with the spectacle of a mountain of dead and
rivers of human blood flowing on the plain. Let us
imagine two armies ready to clash with each other, the
looks of fury, the hideous faces of the soldiers, the
threats, the barbarous cries coming from both sides,
mingled with the thundering of the canon: then the
charge, the frightful mêlée, a slaughter of men, some
dismembered, others half dead and imploring their
comrades to help them by finishing them off so as to
cut short the torment of their miserable, ebbing life.

Afterward, the carnage extends to defenseless people: old men are massacred, children killed or taken prisoner; women are violated, temples profaned; everything is in a
224 state of chaos, and nothing is sure but injustice. And all
this is usually followed by two other evils: famine and pestilence; for, farming having ceased at the onset of the war, the people have no means of feeding themselves and are forced to eat all kinds of meat, good and bad alike. Instead of providing nourishment, it gives rise to corrupt humors, which cause dysentary and other contagious diseases. Alas, Heraclitus was so right in deploring the blindness of man, who brings so many miseries on himself. These miseries make his condition worse than that of the beasts, so that no one need be astonished if Gryllus, after being changed into a pig, preferred to remain in that state rather than to return to his original form. This is why the wise Plotinus was ashamed of being a man and would never speak of his parents or his birth.

Why do we see so many Timons and hermits today? If we accuse them of being misanthropists, they are perfectly within their rights in accusing us in turn of
225 making them that way. The evil, wickedness, and
cruelties that they see every day are enough to make them hate the world. Only an insensitive person could fail to be moved by them. If there were no other consideration than the brevity of our lives and the certainty of death, which threatens us at every moment, we should still be ashamed of torturing ourselves to procure an imaginary honor. We would do better to imitate the example of the Egyptians who brought a skeleton or some other image of death into every

banquet to encourage those present to rejoice and feast while they had the opportunity. But we must aim higher and consider that there is a God who punishes men's sins, especially arrogance and cruelty.

Let us therefore renounce these two vices and wars will cease. We will put the sword back in its scabbard as soon as we have really thought about the emptiness of the reasons for which we take up arms. Let the
Scythians adore the sword. Let us rather emulate the 226
Essenes who did not have an armorer among them, or else the ancient people of Cathay who did not know what it was to kill or do evil. As for me, the only contribution I can make consists of wishes and humble expostulations, which will perhaps be useless. I nevertheless wanted to leave this witness to posterity. If it serves no purpose, have patience. It is a small thing to have wasted paper and words. I shall declare in this case, as Solon did, that I have said and done all I can for the public good. Some who will read this little book will be grateful to me and will honor me, I hope, with their remembrance.

Index

Selected Bibliography

Balch, Thomas Willing. *Eméric Crucé.* Philadelphia: Allen, Lane and Scott, 1900.

Boissonnade, Pierre. *Il primo precursore della società delle nazioni. Il Parigino Emerico Cruce e il suo Nuovo Cinea.* Milan, 1920.

Bonnard, Louis Carle. *Essai sur la conception d'une société des nations avant le XXe siècle.* Thesis, Paris, 1921.

Butler, *Sir* Geoffrey Gilbert. *Studies in Statecraft. Being Chapters Biographical and Bibliographical, Mainly on the Sixteenth Century.* Cambridge: The University Press, 1920.

Crucé, Eméric. *Adonia seu Mnemosynon Henrici Magni. Somnium Philoceltae seu sponsor Cassandrae turcicae. Emerico Cruceo, Parisiensi, auctore.* Paris, 1613.

———. *Emerici Crucei ad P. Papinii Statii Silvas Muscarium sive Helelenchus.* Paris, 1640.

———. *Justa Ludovici Justi, Franciae et Navarrae regis christianissimi. Emericus Cruceus.* Paris, 1642.

———. *Nótae in Statii Thebaïdos.* Paris, 1620.

———. *Le Nouveau Cynée ou Discours d'Estat représentant les occasions et moyens d'establir une paix générale, et la liberté du commerce par tout le monde. Em. Cr. Par.* Paris, 1623.

Le Cinée d'Estat, sur les occurences de ce temps. Aux Monarques et Potentats de ce monde. Par Em. Crucé. Paris, 1624. (This is a second edition of the preceding entry, the only difference between the two being the title.)

———. *The New Cyneas of Eméric Crucé.* Edited with an introduction and translated into English from the original French text of 1623 by Thomas Willing Balch. Philadelphia: Allen, Lane and Scott, 1909.

———. *P. Papinii Statii Silvarum frondatio sive antidiatribe, Emerico Cruceo auctore.* Paris, 1639.

———. *Publii Papinii Statii Opera . . . Emericus Cruceus recensuit.* Paris, 1618.

———. *Soteria Casalea, sive expeditio italica Ludovici Justi.* Paris, 1620.

Crick, Daniel. *Le Nouveau Cynée d'Eméric Crucé.* Bruxelles: Bureau de la Revue, 1910.

Louis-Lucas, Pierre. *Un plan de paix générale et de liberté du commerce au XVIIe siècle: Le Nouveau Cynée d'Eméric Crucé (1623).* Paris: L. Tenin, 1919.

Nys, Ernest. *Etudes de droit international et de droit politique* (1st series, pp. 301-317). Bruxelles: A. Castaigne, Paris: A. Fontemoing, 1896.

Pajot, Jubert. *Un rêveur de paix sous Louis XIII. E. Crucé, Parisien.* Thesis. Paris, 1924.

Regnier, J. *Un précurseur de l'arbitrage international au XVIIe siècle.* Paris, 1903.

Vesnitch, Milan R. *Deux précurseurs français du pacifisme et de l'arbitrage.* Paris: Plon, 1911.

Journal Articles

Nys, Ernest. "Eméric Crucé, l'auteur du 'Nouveau Cynée'," *Revue de droit international et de législation comparée* (2nd series) XI (1909), 594-599.

———. "Histoire littéraire du droit international. A propos de la paix perpétuelle de l'abbé de Saint-Pierre. Eméric Crucé et Ernest, Landgrave de Hesse-Rheinfels," *Revue de droit international et de législation comparée*, XXII (1890), 371-384.

Notes

[1]Translator's note. The *sou* minted at Tours was worth 12 *deniers:* Larousse.

[2]Translator's note. A former coin struck first in the reign of Francis I: Larousse.

[3]We wish to thank Robert H. Land of the Library of Congress, the staff of the British Museum, Roger Pierrot of the *Bibliothèque Nationale*, and J. Chazelas of the *Institut de France* for verifying bibliographical information. C.F.F. and E.R.F.